TURENNE

Marshal of France

TURENNE

HENRI DE LA TOUR D'AUVERGNE, VICOMTE DE TURENNE

TURENNE

Marshal of France

BY
GENERAL MAX WEYGAND

TRANSLATED BY
GEORGE B. IVES

With Illustrations

BOSTON AND NEW YORK
HOUGHTON MIFFLIN COMPANY
The Riverside Press Cambridge
1930

The Riverside Press
CAMBRIDGE · MASSACHUSETTS
PRINTED IN THE U.S.A.

TO THE MEMORY OF
MARSHAL FOCH

It is the nature of noble hearts to discover the essential necessity of the times in which they live and to devote themselves to meeting it.

P. LACORDAIRE

AUTHOR'S NOTE

ALTHOUGH the scheme of this work does not allow the author to cite his sources, he feels bound to acknowledge his obligation to Captain J. Revol's *Psychologie Militaire* and M. C.-G. Picavet's *Les Dernières Années de Turenne*, as well as to documents collected by General Bourelley for a work on Turenne which he has not had time to write.

THE translator has supplied a few footnotes
where they seemed needed to identify persons
mentioned in the text.

CONTENTS

PART I

TURENNE AND RICHELIEU

PART II

TURENNE AND MAZARIN

PART III

TURENNE AND LOUIS XIV

CONTENTS

ILLUSTRATIONS

TURENNE
Marshal of France

. .

PART I
TURENNE AND RICHELIEU

TURENNE
Marshal of France

• •

PART I
TURENNE AND RICHELIEU

CHAPTER I
TURENNE IN THE SERVICE OF FRANCE:
THE HOUSE OF BOUILLON

IN 1629, the Vicomte de Turenne, a young
Huguenot, nineteen years of age, entered the
service of Louis XIII. Hitherto his mother, the
Duchesse de Bouillon, had been unable to reconcile herself to the idea of her sons being in
the French service, so great was her fear that
they might some day be constrained to bear
arms against the followers of the Reformed religion, which Richelieu was seeking to destroy.
A consideration of great weight had led her to
change her mind.

The Duchesse de Bouillon had been obliged,
that same year, to sign a treaty with Richelieu,
whereby she promised to remain always loyal to
the interests of the King of France, who, for his
part, bound himself to take her family under his

3

protection. But shortly after, having had wind of the fact that the far-seeing Cardinal was planning to demand, by way of guaranty, that she should receive a French garrison in Sedan, she no longer hesitated to send her second son, the Vicomte de Turenne, to serve in France, where he would be a hostage for the fulfillment of her pledges to the Crown. In this way she would avoid in the future any arrangements that might be prejudicial to the sovereignty of her older son, the Duc de Bouillon.

And so Turenne entered the service of the King of France in order to safeguard the interests of the House of Bouillon, which he thus learned to place before everything else, and to which he was destined to remain so entirely devoted that he lost one day the true conception of his duty. We must not forget this beginning.

The Cardinal's precautions were certainly not futile. The Duchy of Bouillon and the Principality of Sedan — the 'Sovereign States,' as they were called in those days — were a convenient place of retirement for malcontents, who could foment their intrigues there at their leisure. Wherefore, this territory needed to be watched, and the more narrowly because the character and acts of its last possessor, Henri de La Tour d'Auvergne, father of the marshal to be, were not of a nature to inspire confidence.

Henri de La Tour d'Auvergne was the sixth representative of that branch of the La Tours which, having its source in the cradle of the family, built on the borders of the chain of the Puys, had in 1544 acquired, through marriage, the Viscounty of Turenne, whose domain also marched with Auvergne. Born in 1555, he espoused hotly the cause of Henri of Navarre, whose enterprises he seconded and whose dangers he shared. Of unfailing courage and sound judgment, he combined with his military talents great diplomatic shrewdness, and he was successful in negotiations with Germany and England.

Henri IV, being desirous to show his appreciation of his services, obtained for him the hand of Charlotte de la Mark, who, being heiress to the 'Sovereign States,' was to retain them only on condition that she should marry a Protestant prince 'agreeable' to the King of Navarre. The marriage took place at Sedan, in October, 1591, in the King's presence. By the terms of the contract the Vicomte de Turenne took the titles of Duc de Bouillon and reigning Prince of Sedan and its dependencies.

The bridegroom manifested his gratitude to his sovereign in a fashion which gave the measure of his daring and adventurous character. Stenay being still in the hands of the Leaguers, he

determined to get possession of the place on his
wedding night and give it to the King as a surprise in the morning. He made an excuse to his
royal master for not remaining in direct attendance on his person; then he set out with a force
already under arms, made himself master of the
city, and handed the keys to Henri IV at his
morning reception. '*Ventre-saint-gris!*' cried the
King, 'let me arrange a few such marriages
and I should soon be master of the whole kingdom if all the new bridegrooms would give me
such wedding presents.' Soon after, the Duc
de Bouillon received the bâton of a marshal.

The King had thought that by this marriage
he had placed the Principality of Sedan in the
hands of a loyal retainer of the throne; but that
illusion was to be short-lived. The Duc de
Bouillon was a born conspirator; shrewd, crafty,
and self-willed, he soon found in his King's
abjuration of the Reformed religion an opportunity to practice that genius for intrigue which
had led Richelieu to say of him that 'he could
neither live in peace himself nor let anybody
else.' He took part thenceforth in all the plots
woven against the unity of the kingdom. 'God
preserve me,' said the King, 'from *brouillons*
[meddlers] and Bouillons!'

In 1594, Charlotte de la Mark died without
children. Thereupon the claim of her husband,

surviving her without issue, to possession of the 'Sovereign States,' became more than disputable. The Duc de Bouillon had the audacity to appeal to the King to support his cause. Henri IV agreed, the state of his own affairs compelling him not to be too particular; and thanks to this potent support, the substitution of the House of La Tour d'Auvergne for the House of La Mark in the possession of the 'Sovereign States' was definitively consummated. In the following year the Duc de Bouillon married Elizabeth of Nassau.

The King's kindness was not reciprocated. In 1602, Henri de Bouillon was involved in the conspiracy of Biron; having escaped the capital penalty, which Biron did not escape, he called upon the Huguenots to rise and put Sedan in a state of defense. The King, having summoned him to deliver the city and castle, had no choice, upon his refusal, but to march against his former comrade in arms. He did it with regret. 'I am going to Sedan,' he said, 'with my arms open to receive Monsieur de Bouillon if he chooses; if not, I will teach him his duty.' In March, 1606, the King arrived at Donchery, and then, the Duke having yielded at last, he made his entry into Sedan. He left there a garrison of fifty men which he withdrew a month later, restoring to the rebel, with extraordinary magnanimity, the entire sovereignty over his domains.

Until the death of Henry IV, the Duc de
Bouillon kept quiet. Immediately after that
event he joined the great nobles against Concini,[1] and, being at the head of the Princes'
army, he was declared a rebel. In 1621, the
Assembly of La Rochelle, having decided upon
an uprising, made him general-in-chief. But,
alleging his old age and his health as an excuse,
he refused, and employed the last years of his
life in carrying out the plan of reconstruction
which he had already begun in the Principality.
He died in 1623, leaving it in a state of great
commercial activity, and of excellent public
order and discipline, enriched with a famous
Academy and with a fine library. Being a man
of high culture, and of consummate skill in all
walks of life, but possessed of an ambition which

[1] Concino Concini, Florentine, came to France in the train of
Marie de Médicis, wife of Henri IV. Through his cleverness and
audacity and the influence of his wife, Leonora Galigai, with
Queen Marie, he rose to be first minister in the minority of Louis
XIII, and became the most powerful person in France. He
abandoned the policy of Henri IV and incurred the hatred of all
classes. Became by purchase Marquis d'Ancre. Favored Richelieu's introduction into politics. His unpopularity finally led to
his incurring the disfavor of the King, who ordered his arrest, and
he was killed by the guards while under arrest.

The Princes with whom the Duc de Bouillon joined forces were
Jean-Baptiste Gaston d'Orléans, brother of Louis XIII, and
Henri II de Condé, father of the Great Condé, who is so often
referred to later in the book.

8

shrank from no method of accomplishment, he was deeply involved in all the seditious movements of his time. His conduct fully justified the suspicions of the throne, and it was natural that a watchful eye should be kept on the Principality of Sedan.

The second Duchesse de Bouillon, Elizabeth of Nassau, was a daughter of William the Silent. She was a masterful woman, as ardent a Calvinist as her husband, as clever and ambitious as he, and even more self-willed, if possible. She had given him seven children — two sons and five daughters.

When she was left a widow, she ensured for her sons the manly education that consorted with their rank by sending the young Duc de Bouillon and Vicomte de Turenne to learn the profession of arms in Holland, under their uncles, Maurice and Frederick Henry of Nassau.

Turenne was fifteen years old when he left Sedan. He had none of the brilliant qualities which distinguished his brother. Although of sluggish mind, he had shown himself to be a regular and conscientious worker; but his tutor, the minister Tilenus, declared that he had difficulty in giving utterance to his thoughts and that he was easily confused when he was interrupted. He was enthusiastic over tales of war, he liked to

9

read Cæsar, and was deeply moved by the exploits of Alexander, whom he learned to know in the pages of Quintus Curtius. Although delicate and sickly, he showed a very decided taste for the profession of arms for which his younger-sonship destined him. So he devoted himself vigorously to physical exercises under the direction of his governor, Chevalier de Vassignac. One winter evening, to prove to his friends that he was stout enough to undergo the fatigues of war, he went out secretly and passed the night on the ramparts; they found him in the morning asleep on a gun platform.

The determination and perseverance of which Turenne had thus given proof since his childhood, bore their fruit. He arrived in Holland hardened enough to go through the rough schooling to which his uncle, Maurice of Nassau, subjected him from the outset. This son of William the Silent, of whom it was said that he had 'all the qualities of a man born to found a republic, to discipline an army, and to civilize a nation,' put a musket in Turenne's hands; and he consented cheerfully to pass through the lowest grades and share all the tasks of the common soldier. When Maurice of Nassau died, in 1627, his brother Frederick Henry succeeded him in the government of the Low Countries and in the duty of guiding the destinies of his nephew, to whom he gave the command of a company.

It was at the head of this company that Turenne took part in all his uncle's campaigns, attracting notice by his punctuality and precision, his attention to details, and his solicitude for the welfare of his troops.

In the course of one of his expeditions, he witnessed the death of the Chevalier de Vassignac, and felt his loss keenly. His mother had accustomed him to keep her informed by letter of everything that happened to him; and to this custom, which he continued in later years with his sister and his wife, we owe our knowledge of many of his intimate thoughts, as they were revealed from day to day, with no thought of posterity. Apropos of his governor's death, he wrote his mother a letter which discloses his goodness of heart and his desire to do right: 'I am so extraordinarily distressed by this misfortune that it is impossible for me to think of anything else, and all the things he has said to me recur constantly to my memory. I shall try to put them in practice and shall strive in this way not to disappoint you.'

It was at the siege of Bois-le-Duc, in 1629, that, with several years' experience behind him, he had an opportunity for the first time to show his mettle. Being eager to learn, he was to be found wherever there was any important information to be got. But being, above all else, eager for action, he sought the most hazardous missions; thus it fell to him to place the battery that fired the first guns on the citadel; to construct divers siege works; to carry outlying posts; and to repel the enemy's reconnaissances. In all these tasks he gave proof of great personal courage. The Prince of Orange was proud of his pupil. 'Unless I am very much mistaken,' he said to his staff, 'that young man will some day be the equal of the greatest captains.'

When the troops went into winter quarters, Turenne left Holland and passed the winter, partly at Sedan with his mother, and partly at the French Court, where he found that one of his sisters who was never married, and who used to be called, later, 'Monsieur de Turenne's governess.' From Paris he sent to his mother his impressions of that brilliant society, of the luxury that was universal there, and of every one's desire to advance his own interests. It was evident that he was unhappy there. In the first place, his scanty resources made it necessary for him to reckon before spending, and his letters revealed the precautions that he had to take to retain his social position. He informs us, for instance, that on a certain gala occasion his sister lent him two horses and Madame de Nemours a carriage, and that it was a great convenience to him, otherwise he would have spoiled in the saddle a new coat which had been called very fine.

He had nothing in the way of personal charm to mark him out in the Court circle; nothing in his mentality, which was not alert; nothing in his appearance, which was not fashionable. To be sure, the persistence he had shown in his training and his life passed in camp had given him the manly vigor that he once lacked; but he had no air of distinction. His contemporaries, even those who are most indulgent, agree upon his medium stature, his heavy build, his awkward gait, his broad shoulders, which he raised from time to time in speaking — 'a vile habit which a man usually falls into for lack of self-assurance,' said the spiteful tongue of Bussy-Rabutin. He had a large head and carried it thrust forward a bit, a red complexion, features quite regular but disfigured by thick, bristling eyebrows; the eyes alone were large and beautiful — sometimes flashing fire, they could also glow with extreme softness. While he enjoyed even then a robust constitution, which enabled him to endure so long as he lived the fatigues of war as stoutly as the humblest of his troops, he was never to be an accomplished horseman, if we may believe Mazarin, who, when offering him a few years later two quiet horses, wrote: 'I can ride them

13

perfectly, although I am not a good horseman, and, to speak frankly, you are little better than I.'

And lastly, he was naturally simple in his manner; he knew what was due to his birth, but he was, and was always to remain, entirely devoid of haughtiness and a foe to all useless ostentation. 'I am sending my nephew, Duras, to Court,' he wrote once to his sister; 'you must instruct him as to how he should carry himself; the less show, the better.'

So it was that life at Court, where the name he bore ensured him always a favorable reception, was without charm for him. His family and his soldiers had always the greatest attraction for him.

With nothing notable in his external appearance or in his mental capacity, but manifesting a definite personality by his clearly defined serious tastes and by a perseverance — due to his Auvergnese and Dutch progenitors — which no obstacles could discourage; having already performed military duties which had won him esteem; deeply imbued with the cult of his family; very reserved and difficult of approach for any except his own people — such was this young nobleman of nineteen years whom the interests of the House of Bouillon had forced into the service of the King of France.

CARDINAL DE RICHELIEU

At the moment of his entering that service, Richelieu had already forced upon the Protestants the Peace of La Rochelle and the Peace of Alais,[1] and had cut off the heads of Montmorency-Bouteville, Chalais, and the Maréchal de Marillac. For it was essential for him to strengthen the royal power, so that the King should have nothing to fear within the kingdom when he should come to deal with affairs abroad.

Externally, in truth, matters were going none too well. The Danish period of the Thirty Years' War had ended in the triumph of the Emperor Ferdinand II, who compelled the Protestant princes to restore the property secularized by them since the Peace of Augsburg, threatened the States of the North and the Germanic liberties, and meddled in the affairs of Italy.

Richelieu had promised the King to 'exalt his name among the nations to the height where it should be,' and he entered upon the contest against the House of Austria and Spain. He attacked all their weak points. He seized upon the error committed by the Emperor to raise up against him a formidable foe in Gustavus Adolphus, who undertook the defense of Protestants

---

[1] The Peace of La Rochelle (1628) and the Peace of Alais (1629) were both temporary accommodations between the Crown and the Huguenots.

in Germany. He set about stopping the encroachments of Austria and Holland, protecting the Duchy of Mantua against Spanish and Austrian greed, defending the privileges of Catalonia threatened by Spanish centralization, and restoring the independence of Portugal.

He set about arranging for himself ways of getting into Germany, that he might there support the Emperor's enemies if it should become necessary; and to that end he fortified himself in Metz and pushed forward to Strassburg, and thus punished the Duke of Lorraine for his hostile demonstrations. All of which led to his having armies in Flanders, Italy, Spain, Alsace, Lorraine, and on the Rhine.

It was on these fields of battle that Turenne was to fight and form himself in the years to come.

Chapter II

TURENNE UNDER RICHELIEU:
YEARS OF MILITARY TRAINING

As we are about to follow Turenne in his service in the French armies, it will not perhaps be amiss to say a few words as to those armies and the military art as it was practiced in them.

The principal arm was still the cavalry — an unorganized and undisciplined cavalry, commanded by a body of nobles as unruly as they were fearless. The infantry was already better organized, but it was armed with a musket that took so long to load that the musketeer had to be protected by a pikeman, which made the infantry an unwieldy body and slow in maneuvering. There were cannon, but no artillery, which dates only from Louvois. Engineering was not to appear until Vauban's day; up to then there was only experience to make up for the lack of military engineers. For battle the troops were drawn up in a rigid formation consisting of two lines and a reserve, infantry in the center, cavalry on the wings. The guns were placed in front, to throw the foe into confusion by their fire. The cavalry charged and attempted to turn the flanks.

But they did not fight unless they were fairly

driven to it; for the assailant rarely had the courage to run the risk, and preferred to invest a fortress and acquire the renown of a successful siege. The following words describe very well the strategy of those days: 'One should exhaust all other means of winning before coming to a battle; skillful generals are less anxious to fight battles, where both sides run equal risks, than to destroy the enemy by other means.' It is to be regretted that these words were written at the close of the eighteenth century, for they prove that the totally opposed principles which Turenne left behind him were forgotten when he had gone.

On the other hand, the method of subsistence of the troops had an influence on the conduct of operations. The armies literally lived on the country; at the time of the Treaty of Westphalia, Mazarin congratulated Turenne on 'having done wonders in keeping the army in such good condition without drawing a sou for so long a time.' Hence, the necessity of occupying, at the close of the campaign, a country still rich, 'by means of which we can rehabilitate and reshape an army.' And as soldiers flock to well-equipped armies, they increased the size of their own and diminished that of the enemy, which, 'if we have a little patience, will gradually waste away.'

18

Hence, those long-drawn-out wars, where the final success was won by the slow wearing away of the foe by a combination of military and diplomatic craft with tenacity, and not by sharp and decisive action — a battle such as modern armies seek to bring about. And indeed, upon due reflection, it could not be otherwise: a decisive action, by the combinations which lead up to it, and by the sacrifices it entails, demands from both officers and men a degree of discipline incompatible with the anarchical condition in which France then was; for the discipline of an army is a mirror that reflects the degree of order which reigns in the nation. In proportion as the royal authority became established, discipline came into being, and with it the possibility of a military art less out of date and less passive. Moreover, the age lent itself to such a reorganization; the constantly recurring struggles tended to make men of war perfect in the practice of their profession, and the employment of foreign officers and men in the armies brought about a commingling which was favorable to progress.

Turenne, on his arrival in France to enter the service, was greeted with distinction by the Cardinal and the King, and was given command of a regiment. He devoted all his energies, as he had done with his company in Holland, to making it a fine, well-knit organization. 'My regiment,' he wrote his mother some months later, 'passed before the King to-day; he thought it was very fine and said it was as fine as his own regiment of the Guards.'

At its head he made his first appearance in 1630, in the Army of Italy. Some time after his arrival before the walls of Casale, the campaign ended without a battle. Turenne attributed this fortunate result to the temerarious march of the French troops. We know that the peace was chiefly the work of a young captain, then unknown, who after a very eventful life had taken service with Pope Urban VIII; his name was Mazarin. The Sovereign Pontiff, desiring to make an end of this new war, had sent an embassy of which Mazarin was a member; and he did so well by running from one belligerent to another to induce a cessation of hostilities, that he succeeded in persuading them to accept a compromise, which resulted in the Treaty of Cherasco. Mazarin signed it; it was the first step in his upward career. Thus Turenne and Mazarin, whose collaboration was destined to do so much for the grandeur of France, stepped together upon the stage of history before the walls of Casale.

Until 1634, Turenne divided his time between France and Holland, which had become allies.

In that year he definitively quitted the service of Holland and served in the Army of Lorraine under Maréchal de La Force, whose granddaughter he was, later, to marry. He distinguished himself at the siege of La Motte. A breach having been made in the main bastion, La Force threw in the regiment of his son, the Marquis de Tonneins, which was driven back. The next day came Turenne's chance, and all eyes were turned upon the young colonel. He marched up to the breach in the face of an extremely hot fire; his calmness and gallantry inspired his troops, who drove the enemy from the bastion, and La Motte fell shortly after. As the result of this brilliant action Turenne was made brigadier-general.

The following year found him with the Army of the Rhine, under the orders of the Cardinal de La Valette, and it was in the confusion of a hurried retreat that his military talents really revealed themselves for the first time. The Cardinal de La Valette had rashly crossed the Rhine; cut off by the Imperial troops, he was compelled to retire in haste behind the river, and then beyond the Sarre. He had to bury his guns and begin a retreat which lasted fourteen days and imposed incredible hardships on the troops. Turenne shared with his soldiers such food as he could find. He had everything superfluous removed from his carriages, to make room for the wounded to ride. One day, seeing one of the poor devils lying exhausted at the foot of a tree, he gave him his horse and went forward on foot until he found a carriage in which he could put him. It was that march that gave him the name, which spread throughout the army, of 'father' of his troops.

In 1636, with the Army of Alsace, Turenne was seriously wounded in the arm before Saverne — so seriously that for a short time it was feared that amputation would be necessary, and there was profound anxiety concerning the fate of this youth who was beginning to make his name known.

But he made a quick recovery and fought in 1637 in the Army of Flanders. The siege of Landrecies was especially difficult, the soldiers being obliged to live in trenches half full of water. Turenne held them to their duty by his own example, and when the younger ones had reached the point where they could hold out no longer, he induced the veterans, by liberal gifts, to hold the trenches out of turn. It was in this campaign that Turenne had occasion to test the high quality of Fabert, to whom he was later united in the bonds of devoted friendship.

In 1638, Turenne returned to the Army of Alsace, this time under the command of Bernard of Saxe-Weimar. We must pause a moment to speak of this general, who had a decisive influence on the formation of Turenne's character. 'He would make something out of nothing and not be puffed up by his success; when he had a bit of ill fortune, he thought not so much of whining about it as of recovering from it, being more intent upon redeeming his mistakes than upon wasting his time in excuses; in a word, he tried harder to make his men love him than to make them fear him.' It was thus that Turenne expressed himself about him in words that came to apply so closely to himself a few years later.

The Duke of Saxe-Weimar's military genius bore the impress of Gustavus Adolphus, who, in that first half of the seventeenth century, left so vivid an impression that his name was often invoked by military officers. They would say, speaking of a successful stroke, 'The King of Sweden would have done it so'; just as the military men of our day refer to Napoleon. By introducing a somewhat lighter firearm, more flexible formations, more mobile artillery, and by encouraging the initiative of his subordinate officers, Gustavus Adolphus had been able to carry out the bold and swiftly executed tactics to which he owed his success. Bernard of Saxe-Weimar was his favorite pupil; he took command of the Swedish army at the battle of Lutzen after the King had been mortally wounded. Afterward he was invited by Richelieu to place his talents at the service of France, and it was through him that the ideas of the King of Sweden found their way thither. Turenne remained but a short time under Duke Bernard's orders, but he was deeply influenced by him.

In this campaign of 1638, Turenne distinguished himself at Ensisheim, where he surprised the Emperor's army in its camp. Then, by a swift maneuver, he advanced upon Brisach, attacked with four hundred men the last fortress that still resisted, cut down the palisade with axes, forced an entrance in two places at once, and compelled the surrender of the place.

In the two following years Turenne was again in Italy. At first he joined the Cardinal de La Valette, and crowned himself with glory in the fight on the road to Quiers — a stoutly contested action — in company with Fabert. In 1640, under the Vicomte d'Harcourt, there was the raising of the siege of Casale, in the course of which Turenne completely routed four thousand enemy horsemen. And there was Moncaliere, where, as his troops were about crossing a stream swollen by rains, he threw himself into the flood, crossed it, drew them after him, and dislodged the foe. And, finally, there was the siege of Turin, an extraordinary spectacle: the citadel, which was occupied by the French, was besieged by Prince Thomas of Savoy, who was master of the city, but was himself besieged by the French army, which was, in its turn, besieged by the Spanish army. Doubtless this strange concatenation of circumstances inspired the poet when he wrote:

> Rien de plus compliqué que ce siège d'Arras:
> Nous assiégeons Arras, nous-mêmes, pris au piège,
> Le Cardinal Infant d'Espagne nous assiège —
> Quelqu'un devrait venir l'assiéger à son tour! [1]

Turenne was wounded by a musket-ball. He dressed his own wound and returned in time to help in the reduction of the place. And so, while the Vicomte d'Harcourt returned to France to rest, Turenne, by order of the Court, took command of the Army of Italy.

He was now thirty years of age. He had lived for ten years a distinguished, purely military life, devoted to his profession, and preferring such sober satisfaction to that which he might readily have enjoyed at Court. His gallantry was acknowledged by all, his talents were beginning to become matured, his solicitude and affection for his troops — a rare thing in those days — assured their devotion. He had completed his

---

[1] Nothing could be more complicated than this siege of Arras: we are besieging Arras, and the Cardinal Infante of Spain is besieging us, who are caught in a trap. Now some one ought to come and besiege him in his turn.

education as a subordinate officer. He acknowledged, with the modesty which is one of the
essential features of his character, all that he
owed to his teachers, which Napoleon summa-
rized thus:

'He had served under four generals: the Prince
of Orange, his uncle, to whom he said that he
owed his rules for choosing a camp wisely and
assaulting a fortress properly; the Duke of
Weimar, of whom he said that he made everything out of nothing; the Cardinal de La Valette,
from whom he had learned to turn his back on
the false refinements of the Court and on the
philandering there, and to adopt the tone of the
camp; and the Comte d'Harcourt, from whom
he learned that diligence and activity are the
greatest sources of success in the affairs of war.'

Surely a magnificent beginning that; and
Turenne in his passionate love of arms would
have been a perfectly happy man had not his
brother's conduct given him serious cause for
anxiety.

The Duc de Bouillon had in fact inherited his
father's ambition and love of intrigue. In 1634,
despite the opposition of his kindred, he had
married Eleonore of Bergues, a woman of noble
birth, great beauty, and lofty intellect, but of the
Catholic faith. He fell so entirely under her

26

influence that Fabert said of him, 'There's a man whose wife is his soul.' The fact is that, being deeply impressed by his wife's virtues, he conceived doubts on the subject of the religion he had always professed, and after two years of study and reflection he abjured Calvinism.

This shift of religion did not put an end to his habitual intriguing. A letter from Turenne to his mother tells much about it in a few words: 'I did not see the Cardinal until day before yesterday, and yesterday I saw the King. The former said to me that it was necessary that my brother should speak frankly to him, and that, if he did, he would stand sponsor for him to the King. He said also, "You won't go to the Bastille this time, but do not keep on doing as you have done."' Thus we learn at one and the same time that the Duc de Bouillon was incorrigible, and that his hostage was really held answerable for the loyalty of the family.

In 1641, the Comte de Soissons fell out with Richelieu and withdrew to Sedan, where the Duc de Bouillon gave him shelter. The Cardinal ordered him to turn his enemy over to him. The Duc de Bouillon refused, and so broke with the Cardinal in his turn. The Spaniards naturally took the part of the malcontents. Henri II of Guise, Archbishop of Rheims, joined them at Sedan. A treaty was concluded with the Emperor, and behold the Principality had become once more a center of intrigues against France. Richelieu proposed to attack and destroy the fortress of Sedan, but 'the Army of the Princes' whipped the royal army at La Marfée. However, as the Comte de Soissons was killed there, everything was smoothed over and the Duke obtained his pardon and retained his estates and his privileges, thanks chiefly to Cinq-Mars, the King's first equerry and favorite.

In the following year Cinq-Mars and De Thou got up a conspiracy of their own, to overthrow Richelieu, and entered into treasonable negotiations with Spain. The Cardinal obtained a copy of the treaty; he found proof therein of the complicity of Turenne's brother, and had him arrested, together with the two chief culprits, in the Army of Italy of which he had just been given the command.

Turenne, recently made lieutenant-general, was serving at this time in the Army of Spain. He was before Perpignan when he learned, we can imagine with what distress, of his brother's arrest. 'Never in my life,' he wrote Madame de Bouillon, 'have I had any news that moved me so deeply as that my brother had been arrested by the King's order. They write me from the Court that it is quite certain that my brother took part in this conspiracy of Monsieur le

Grand,[1] and Monsieur le Cardinal has written me that he will show me how my brother, only two months after his submission, had already begun to mix in this business. Seeing what all this means, I have implored my brother a hundred times, when I returned from Sedan to Paris, to take heed to himself and do nothing that could arouse suspicion.'

Cinq-Mars and De Thou were executed. The Bouillon family interceded for its chief, who proposed to restore Sedan, 'the cause of all his misfortunes,' in exchange for other estates. Richelieu was too shrewd not to prefer the Principality to the Prince's head. A pardon, and an order to turn over the city and castle, set the conspirator free. Sedan was occupied by the King's troops; on the very day that they entered, the old Duchesse de Bouillon died from shock, and from wrath, too, no doubt; at all events, the inexorable woman was spared the shame of witnessing this consecration, as it were, of the debasement of her House, which she had done so much to avert.

Fabert became Governor of Sedan. When the post was offered him, he asked leave, before accepting it, to consult Turenne, who replied: 'If my family is compelled to give up Sedan,

[1] Monsieur le Grand was the title ordinarily given to Gaston d'Orléans, brother of Louis XIII.

I prefer to see the place in your hands rather than any other officer's' — a remark which does the one as much honor as the other.

Richelieu died December 4, 1642, before he had had time to arrange the selection of the estates which the King had consented to give the Duc de Bouillon in exchange for his principality. The settlement of this perplexing question was destined to be dragged out to interminable length — a fact which gave rise to serious differences between Turenne and Mazarin.

PART II

TURENNE AND MAZARIN

PART II
TURENNE AND MAZARIN

CHAPTER I
TURENNE UNDER CONDÉ:
TURENNE COMMANDER-IN-CHIEF

LOUIS XIII soon followed Richelieu to the grave. He died May 14, 1643, having named Mazarin as one of the four advisers of the Regent [Queen Anne of Austria]. She forced the Parliament to annul the will which limited her powers, and selected Mazarin as First Minister.

A tremendous task remained to be accomplished, complicated by a mass of difficulties inherent in the King's minority.[1] Mazarin set about its accomplishment, continuing his predecessor's policy with equal determination, but by an altogether different method. 'This successor of the formidable Cardinal,' wrote De Retz, 'mild and benignant as he was, wanting nothing, and in despair because his dignity as a cardinal forbade him to be as humble as he would have liked,

---

[1] Louis XIV was born in 1638 and succeeded to the throne in 1643 at the age of five. When he assumed personal control of the government at Mazarin's death, he was twenty-three years old.

played his cards so well that he found himself over everybody's head when everybody thought that he was still by his side.'

Like Richelieu, and falling into the same inevitable contradiction, he sought in his contest against the House of Austria alliances with the Protestant princes of Germany at the same time that he was at work within France to annihilate the Huguenots. To this end he strove to decapitate the party by inducing its leaders to go over to Catholicism. He succeeded with the Maréchal de Rantzau, but failed with the Maréchal de Gassion, of whom he says in his secret notes that 'we must keep an eye on him and make sure that he does not try to lead the Huguenot party.'

Did he try a similar game with Turenne? We might think so when we read in these same notes the opinion, of the same tenor, that the Cardinal held of him: 'People think, and he thinks it too, that the whole Protestant party regards him as a rising sun and as a man destined to bring the Huguenots within his beams. It is necessary to observe this man closely, because beyond doubt he has far-reaching plans in his mind.'

Did Turenne in fact harbor such far-reaching plans? His contemporaries are agreed as to his reserve, and to get at his private thoughts we must question the letters written to his usual

34

CARDINAL MAZARIN

confidants. Do we discover therein any traces of the ambition which so disturbed Mazarin?

In a letter written a few months before the death of Louis XIII, he says to his sister that the King uses the pretext of his religion to show that he proposes to do nothing for him. He recurs frequently to the adjustment of his brother's affairs, 'with whom,' he writes, 'it is painful to see that the Queen and Monsieur [the late King's brother] are omnipotent, and that we have lost Sedan for love of them' — hardly the remark of a courtier. 'We must be very careful,' he says more than once, 'to ask nothing for me, my brother's business not being settled.' And when Cardinal Mazarin offered him the Duchy of Château-Thierry, he replied that he would accept nothing so long as the Duc de Bouillon had not received satisfaction.

But at the same time, he writes: 'This business does not diminish in the least my affection and loyalty to the service; I feel that I have given such strong proof of that, that it is useless for me to assert it.' And again, 'I am more negligent of my own affairs than I have ever been, and the King has a very good servant in me; for provided I do what I can to rebuild this army, it seems to me that things will go very well with me.' We could multiply such passages indefinitely. What are we to conclude from them? That Turenne placed what he owed to his family before all else? He disapproves his brother's conduct, but he remains loyal to him as head of the House of Bouillon, to witness the grandeur of which is his highest ambition. Personal ambition comes only second, and is exclusively military; still he seems to give it a place, especially in the performance of his duties.

The first mission that Mazarin entrusted to Turenne was to go to Italy and conduct, under the orders of Thomas of Savoy, operations which resulted in the siege and capture of Trino. On his return to Paris, he was created a marshal of France. Was the government of Anne of Austria fearful that its dilatoriness in adjusting the affairs of the Duc de Bouillon would offend Turenne, and that the Protestants would make it a pretext for manifesting their discontent; and did it seek by this step to allay such suspicions? We may attribute to designs such as these a share in the bestowal of this distinction; but surely it was a legitimate reward for such brilliant service, even then of long duration.

In this year 1643 France had undergone a serious setback on the Rhine. Rantzau, who had succeeded the Maréchal de Guébriant who was killed at Rothweil, had been beaten and captured at Dutlingen and the Weimar troops were dis-

banded. The Imperial officials made so much
noise over this success that they caused Rocroi [1]
to be forgotten. This eclipse of French prestige
came at an unfortunate time, for Osnabrück
and Münster had just received plenipotentiaries
who were destined to discuss terms of peace for
five years, and it was desirable that arms should
come to the rescue of diplomacy.

Under these circumstances the Cardinal put
aside his suspicions and named Turenne to take
command of the Army of Germany. He wrote
on this occasion to his plenipotentiaries, MM.
Servien and d'Avaux, a letter which we should
like to quote in full: 'Since success in arms is
never constant, I write you sincerely and truth-
fully of our ill fortune, which is not so great as
one might imagine, and which will be so fully
repaired a month hence that I hope that nothing
of it will remain but the memory.'

He goes on to advise them of the choice made
by the Queen of the Vicomte de Turenne to
command the army, and of his speedy arrival
with excellent troops and plenty of money. And
he closes thus: 'I say nothing to you of the
merits of M. de Turenne, who, in addition to his
high birth by which he is connected with the

---

[1] The battle of Rocroi was fought during the first stage of the
Thirty Years' War by the French under Condé, then Duc
d'Enghien, against the Spaniards, in May, 1643.

37

greatest houses of Germany, and in addition to his rank as Marshal of France, with which the Queen has recently honored him, and his general reputation in his profession, has served a long time in Germany with the very forces he is now to command, by whom we know that he is loved and admired as he deserves to be; and so we can promise ourselves that our lost prestige and advantages will speedily be recovered under such a leader, and that whatever surprise our allies may feel at first will soon disappear.'

How can one fail to admire the minister who confronts adversity with such lofty calmness; who, overcoming his prejudices, calls upon the leader whom he deems most capable, and points out so fairly the reasons for his choice and his grounds for hope? It was at this moment that the collaboration of Turenne and Mazarin began; their mutual understanding was broken by spasms of suspicion, often justified on one side or the other, for they lived in a terribly confused and discordant time when one's duty was perhaps more difficult to discover than to perform. But, as they came to know each other better, the mutual confidence between those two great servants of the State was to grow closer and closer until, at the time of the Cardinal's death, it was without a rift.

The Marshal started out at once. He was

cordially welcomed by the Weimarites, Protestants like himself, who knew in what high esteem their chief, Duke Bernard, held him. At this juncture something happened which revealed Turenne's character clearly enough. The Duke of Saxe-Weimar had made M. d'Erlach governor of Brisach. He, offended by being put under Turenne, left the place before his arrival and retired to a country house of his in Switzerland. 'M. de Turenne,' says Turenne in his Memoirs, 'was a little surprised by M. d'Erlach's action in quitting so fine a position on the strength of an unfounded suspicion; but thinking that it would be unworthy of him to take advantage of this act to get control of his government, he sent M. de Tracy to him to ask him to return.' D'Erlach returned, but unreformed; for a few years later, his susceptibility having again taken offense, Turenne wrote to his sister: 'I have fallen out altogether with M. d'Erlach; he doesn't answer the letters I write him and has returned his commission as lieutenant-general. This will compel me to treat his friends better and give him no excuse for remaining angry.' Sentiments of an unusual type these!

Turenne did a great job of reorganization in the Army of Germany, and to put it on its feet once more, he was obliged to make personal sacrifices and to borrow large sums of money.

He restored discipline. He visited the forts in Alsace and strengthened their defenses. So that, in the spring of 1644, he was at the head of an excellent army, strongly entrenched. At Donaueschingen he won a victory over the Bavarians, which, with a modesty on which Mazarin complimented him, he was content to announce as 'ordinary'; but he could not prevent Mercy from taking Fribourg. Just then the Duc d'Enghien[1] was on the way, with strong reënforcements, to take command of the army, and Turenne wrote to Mazarin: 'If M. d'Enghien is to command the reënforced army, I shall deem myself highly honored to serve under him and I shall obey him as I ought.'

A few days later the Duc d'Enghien attacked the Bavarians at Fribourg — a desperate conflict which ended, after several days of fighting, by the precipitate retreat of the Bavarians, who abandoned their guns and impedimenta. The Duc d'Enghien, in his report, declares that during those severe battles Turenne acted 'with all possible courage and skill.' The campaign ended with the capture of Fribourg, where Turenne commanded one of the assaults. After which, the Duc d'Enghien having returned to

[1] The title borne before his father's death in 1646 by Louis II de Bourbon, 'the Great Condé,' under which title we shall hear much of him later.

France with a goodly share of the army, he went on to undertake with a small force the duty of preventing the enemy from crossing the Rhine.

He remained on the spot all winter. But the campaign of 1645 began badly. Being called upon by the Swedes, Turenne crossed the Rhine, then the Neckar, and went into camp at Marienthal. He fell into a trap that Mercy laid for him, and left the Weimar troops in widely scattered cantonments. Mercy then fell upon him and defeated him completely, capturing a large part of his infantry, all his impedimenta, twelve guns, and twelve hundred cavalry. Turenne himself was very nearly taken. He had the presence of mind, however, not to fall back directly upon the Rhine: he so directed his retreat as to threaten the enemy's flank if he should attempt to march to the river; the Landgrave of Hesse placed his troops under his command, and the affair ended without very great harm being done.

To understand a man thoroughly, one must have seen him when fortune was adverse; at this juncture Turenne showed as much frankness as nobility of character. He did not try to minimize the importance of his defeat; he even offered to resign his command. But the Cardinal generously assured him that in the position of extreme danger in which he had been placed, he had taken the best and most honorable course.

From his letters to his sister concerning 'the disaster that had befallen him,' one realizes how deeply he was distressed by it.

Soon after, the Duc d'Enghien arrived with more than ten thousand men, and took over the command. At Nordlingen he attacked Mercy, who was entrenched there in a strong position. The battle was a desperate one, 'the greatest that we have seen since the war began,' writes Turenne. The Duc d'Enghien performed prodigies of valor; he had two horses killed under him and was thrice wounded; but he could make no progress against the Bavarian infantry in the center, while his right wing was enveloped. Thereupon he threw Turenne in on the left against Weinberg, which he took, and by quick maneuvering threatened the Bavarian right. Darkness came on and the battle was still undecided when Mercy was killed, and that brought about the retreat of his army. After the victory, the Duc d'Enghien wrote to Mazarin: 'M. le Maréchal de Turenne did incredible things in this affair, and but for his most extraordinary courage and military skill, the battle would have been lost.' Whereas Turenne wrote to his sister: 'I cannot describe what M. le Duc d'Enghien did on this occasion by dint of his personality, his courage, and his leadership.'

The Duc d'Enghien having fallen ill, so ill

that he had to give up the command of the army,
the Bavarians joined the Emperor and Turenne
recrossed the Rhine. But shortly after, taking
advantage of a blunder of the enemy, he made
a forced march of forty leagues upon Trèves,
invested and took the city, and reinstated the
Elector. Mazarin congratulated him upon bringing the campaign to so glorious a close.

After a few weeks at Court, Turenne rejoined
his troops at Mayence in April, 1646. He was
preparing to cross the Rhine to join the Swedes,
when the Cardinal ordered him not to do so. It
will be remembered that negotiations were proceeding side by side with the military operations;
the Duke of Bavaria had been shrewd enough
to assure the representatives of Münster that he
would not join the Emperor if the French remained on the west side of the Rhine; hence the
Cardinal's decision. Turenne, who knew his
Germans, knew that by following this course we
should seriously jeopardize our interests, but he
did not cross the Rhine, 'in order not to act so
hastily in contravention of an express command.'
Soon after, he learned that the armies of the
Emperor and the Duke of Bavaria had come
together and were marching against the Swedes.
Thereupon, taking nobody's advice but his own,
he left a skeleton force at Mayence, and, sending
word to the Cardinal, determined to cross the

river at Wesel, eighty leagues from where he
then was. The march took fourteen days. He
crossed the river, ascended the right bank, and
joined Wrangel and the Swedes.

At Wesel, Turenne had a never-to-be-forgotten
experience. In those days, as to-day, the fair
sex loved to show themselves in those places
where the fate of nations was being decided, and
the Duchesse de Longueville happened to be
passing through the town on her way to join the
Duke, who was coming from Münster to meet
her. Was it then that Turenne felt the first
touch of a sentiment which, to his misfortune,
was to grow to such proportions some years
later? 'My dear sister, I crossed the Rhine
yesterday at Wesel. Madame de Longueville
arrived there the same day, and came to-day to
see the army. From here we shall go on together
for a day or two. I confess that there is nobody
on earth so wonderful. She has not changed at
all.' That is what he tells us; it is enough for us
to picture the fascinating Duchess as she appears
in the word-portrait that Madame de Motteville
has left of her: 'She had an admirable figure; her
whole personality had an attraction whose power
extended even to her own sex. It was impossible
to see her without loving her and longing to
please her. And yet her beauty consisted rather
in the coloring of her face than in perfection of

ANNE GENEVIÈVE DE BOURBON, DUCHESSE DE LONGUEVILLE

feature. Her eyes were not large, but lovely, soft, and bright, and of an adorable shade of blue — it was like the blue of a turquoise. Poets could find no other comparison than lilies and roses for the white and red of her face, and her fair hair, touched with silver, made her much more like an angel than a woman.' An eye-witness described her 'standing in a chariot drawn by six horses with crimson velvet trappings, richly embroidered,' and the army of the Vicomte de Turenne passing in review before her, 'the cavalry by squadrons, with their guidons on one side of the road and on the other the trumpets blowing and drums beating. Then came the infantry in perfect alignment, with banners displayed and drums beating in each company. Finally, when M. de Turenne came to take leave of their Highnesses, the whole force fired a volley and made a deuce of a noise.'

This pleasant interlude did not delay the junction of the two allied armies, which together formed a force of seventeen thousand men. The enemy's strength was half as many more, but the Marshal went about his operations with a determination and activity commensurate with the audacity of his initial maneuver. He crossed the Main, marched to the Danube, which he crossed, taking advantage of the ill-advised movements of the Archduke Leopold to carry

45

the war into Bavaria. He reached the Lech at
Augsburg, and seized the Archduke's stores,
thus forcing him to return in hot haste to Austria. Maximilian of Bavaria, abandoned by his
allies, was fain to accept the Peace of Ulm.
Napoleon, in his comments on Turenne's campaigns, is more enthusiastic about this one of
1646 than any other; he praises without reserve
the Marshal's initiative and the audacity, good
judgment, and skill of his maneuvers.

The Cardinal would have liked to profit by
these great successes in Germany to withdraw
the army therefrom, fearing to destroy the
Catholic religion there if he should crush the
Emperor. Turenne believed, on the contrary,
that we should hold a portion of Germany in
order not to leave the Duke of Bavaria in control
of affairs. But the year 1647 opened under evil
auspices: the defection of the United Provinces
left us alone in the Low Countries face to face
with Spain, and it became necessary to send
troops thither. In vain did Turenne insist that
his German cavalry would raise objections to
following him, because five or six months' pay
was due them — he received repeated orders,
one in the Queen's own hand, to take his army
into Flanders, so he crossed the Rhine again.
But at Saverne, the Weimar troops refused to
go farther unless they were paid in full, which

was impossible, Mazarin having sent no money.

A German officer, Lieutenant-General Rosen, encouraged the mutineers and started with them for Strassburg. He was already crossing the river when Turenne, having marched ten leagues in a day, overtook him. Seeing how far things had gone, and realizing how greatly the Army of Flanders was in need of reënforcements, he sent thither the troops who had remained loyal to him, and without hesitation, at the risk of his own safety, with only twelve men among all the rebels, he marched with them, striving to bring them back to their duty. He continued along the river as far as Philipsburg, without making any impression. Then, having come within range of that place, he summoned one hundred musketeers during the night, had Rosen seized and bound, and sent him to prison at Nancy. This audacious stroke succeeded: nearly all the mutineers declared for the Marshal; only fifteen hundred of them went into Bavaria with the officers they had chosen. Turenne pursued and attacked them, killed three hundred and took three hundred more, and the rest disbanded. This affair, in which he showed no less patience than presence of mind, being brought to a close, he started for Flanders.

But his anticipations, alas! were realized: the Duke of Bavaria, once more a traitor, had joined the Imperial forces and repulsed the Swedes. The Court had to order Turenne into Germany; but it was so late in the season that it was impossible for him to effect anything.

With his customary activity he reconditioned his army, and then, to prove that France does not allow herself to be flouted with impunity, he declared to the Duke of Bavaria that he proposed to treat him as an enemy, and early in 1648 he crossed the Rhine yet again and joined the Swedes.

Once the allies were reunited, certain points of disagreement arose between them, 'regarding a multitude of trifles which it would take too long to write about.' Trifles appeared of less and less importance in his eyes, for so far as the important things were concerned, thanks to his character which acquired greater firmness every day, the authority of his opinion imposed itself on his allies.

Without the loss of a day, Turenne drove the Imperial army south of the Danube, overtook at Susmarshausen its rear-guard, commanded by Montecuculli, defeated it, and forced Melander, his commander-in-chief, to turn back to support him in a battle in which Melander was killed. Turenne pursued instantly, surprised the troops crossing the Isar, forced the Bavarian Court to abandon Munich, and reached the Inn, thus marking out the road for the troops of

Austerlitz. And so Napoleon wrote: 'Turenne was the first French general to plant the national colors on the banks of the Inn. In this campaign and in that of 1646, he overran Germany in all directions, with a mobility and daring in strong contrast to the way in which war has been waged since.'

If we cast an eye over the five years that had passed since his commission as Marshal of France had summoned Turenne to the chief command, we observe that he had grown tremendously. Doubtless he was, and was content to be, only second to Condé, when the latter wrote pages of his dazzling epic at Fribourg and Nordlingen. But for the first time he had had a chance to take part in decisions of high military policy, and we have seen what sureness of judgment he had shown. In the vast domains of Germany, which he had overrun victoriously, his horizon had widened. He had learned how to make use of time and space, and had passed his apprenticeship in the wars of coalitions. In this new school, by unremitting toil, he was eventually to become superior to his rival in the general conduct of war. 'In speaking of a single campaign, we speak more enthusiastically of what Monsieur le Prince [Condé] did; but when it is over, we enjoy longer the fruits of what M. Turenne did,' Saint-

Évremond was to write later, and very truly. On the other hand, his character had become stronger. Now he announced and supported his opinions, whatever the Court might think about it; he sought the initiative, and showed himself to be as upright and stout of heart in misfortune as he was modest in success. However, he did not fail to realize in his own heart the quality of his services, for if he does declare with entire sincerity that 'in war the most clever are simply they who make the fewest mistakes'; and if he replies to those who extol his victories, 'You forget that I was beaten at Marienthal'; nevertheless he writes to Madame de Bouillon, when the success of his maneuver of 1646 was becoming manifest, 'Thank God, the affair is proceeding on a grand scale!' The phrase already applies to himself.

Turenne's successes in Germany and Condé's victory at Lens constrained the House of Austria to make peace, which was at last ratified at Münster and Osnabrück. It was the Treaty of Westphalia, 'which settled for a century public law in Europe.'

But Spain held aloof from the treaty; she knew that disorder was increasing in France, and that, as in the days of the League, she would find her profit in it. Unhappily her foresight was too accurate.

CHAPTER II

THE FRONDE:
THE MISTAKE AND THE RECOVERY

THE external successes of the government passed
unnoticed amid the general discontent that prevailed within the kingdom. France was threatened by civil war, and the Fronde [1] was to bring
Turenne face to face with a moral crisis in which
one might wish that he had chosen a different
course. But we must refrain from passing judgment upon his conduct according to present-day
ideas.

Patriotism at that time was not even a definite
conception. Loyalty to the king was the sole
duty of the great, in so far as the monarch's
authority did not encroach upon privileges which
had their source, doubtless, in that authority,
but which, according to the still existent feudal
tradition, marked its natural limits. 'The duty
of the princes of the blood,' writes Retz, 'is to go

---

[1] The Fronde is the name given in the first place to the party
which waged civil war against the Court party during the
minority of Louis XIV; and in the second place it is generally
applied to the conflict itself, which continued from 1648 to 1652,
when Mazarin was driven from power. He was soon restored,
however, after the opposition to him had become a mere matter
of selfish intrigue.

to war rather than surrender anything of their dignity.'

The politics of the time took no heed of the nationality of those who served the king. The Swiss D'Erlach, a Swedish colonel, was Governor of Brisach; the German Schomberg and the Dane Rantzau were marshals of France; Bernard of Saxe-Weimar led the king's troops against his own land. Finally, the Italian Mazarin was First Minister of the Regent.

Public opinion made a clear distinction between the latter and the King [Louis XIV]. The Cardinal's unpopularity was reflected upon the Queen, who had raised him to the highest rank. And in 1645, at Notre Dame, women threw themselves at her feet, imploring her to dismiss 'that man who is laying his hands on everything.'

It is, therefore, perfectly easy to understand that devotion to the King should marshal the public authorities against the authority of the Regent. The Parliament of Paris, declaring war on Mazarin, inscribed on its banners: '*Querimus regem nostrum*' [We want our King], and wrote to the youthful monarch: 'Your preservation, Sire, and that of the realm are the sole causes of our action and the reasons for our decree ordering Paris to take up arms.'

Under the last reign, men had seen the father of the Great Condé acclaimed at Paris as the enemy of Concini, and all France conniving at the assassination of that alien minister; the Queen-Mother, Marie de Médicis, fighting against the royal troops on the Pont-de-Cé, and being driven at last to seek asylum in the Low Countries. And Anne of Austria herself — had not she conspired with Spain against Richelieu? These so recent events made it possible to believe in good faith that a regent, assisted by a foreign-born minister, might act in contravention of the King's interests.

This state of mind was expressed by Turenne himself in writing to the Queen: 'Monsieur d'Orléans [1] and Monsieur le Prince are entitled to propose to you whatever they think essential to the well-being of the State, and their mouths cannot be closed.'

However, the Duc de Bouillon and Turenne were 'foreign princes'; that is to say, they possessed sovereign estates outside of France. Turenne had been placed in the King's service as a hostage in pledge for that sovereignty. He was in France, therefore, only by authority of the head of his house, obedience to whom, according to the political principles of the day, was his highest duty.

[1] The Duc d'Orléans, oldest brother of Louis XIV. The oldest brother was generally spoken of as 'Monsieur' simply. 'Monsieur le Prince' is Condé.

Now, since the Duc de Bouillon had sacrificed his estates in order to escape the loss of his head, he had fought unceasingly to recover the rights and privileges which he had been forced to renounce. Disappointed by the steps taken at the outset of the new reign, he had plotted in Italy with the agents of Spain, while at Brussels the Duchess was working against France. This did not incline Mazarin to give him satisfaction, and Turenne maintained before the Cardinal the interests of his family. Their private correspondence in the years preceding the Fronde revolves about this subject. 'I am told,' Turenne writes, 'that Your Excellency complains that I do not respond to your friendship for me. I beg you to give some proofs of it to our family.'

Mazarin tried in vain to open his eyes to his brother's conduct, 'who is too far over the precipice to be able to draw back'; and to that of his sister-in-law, 'who has pushed him over and is not ready to help him out.' In vain did he urge him to have no further relations with that enemy of the State, reminding him of the Queen's kindness, which had raised him to his present height, and her confidence that he would remain true to her. Time passed and they could arrive at no mutual understanding.

At the close of the year 1648, we find Turenne greatly exasperated with the Cardinal. In his

letters to his sister he declares that he must have
a settlement for his family and something definite
for himself; that he prefers to be altogether at
odds with the Court rather than accept any post
which he cannot honorably retain; that he must
not fear results, but let that happen which God
wills. Thus we see that he, too, was on the brink
of the precipice.

In the early days of 1649, Paris, incited by the
Parliament, flew to arms, and the Court, still
strong in the support of Condé, retired to Saint-
Germain. Mazarin realized the necessity of
making sure of Turenne's loyalty. The banker
Herwarth, whose mission it was to pay the arrears due the troops, and Ruvigny, a kinsman of
Turenne, plied to and fro between Court and
army. The Queen wrote thrice with her own
hand to the Marshal, to show her confidence
and affection. But, on the other hand, the Cardinal was negotiating with the Weimarian troops,
to attach them to his cause, in case Turenne
should yield to 'the tricks that his brother might
resort to,' and went so far as to arrange with
D'Erlach and Herwarth for the Marshal's arrest.
He learned of the plan, and in his indignation
refused the government of Upper and Lower
Alsace. 'To accept higher rank in all these
bargainings,' he wrote to Condé, 'would seem
as if I sought to profit by the misfortunes of

others.' And to the Queen, 'I am most unfortunate in that favors come to me only at times when I cannot accept them, that is, when my brother is out of favor with Your Majesty.' Thus we find Turenne deliberately sacrificing all personal rewards to his older brother's interest.

His mind was made up. He issued a manifesto to his troops, asking them to return with him to France. At the same time the Parliament of Paris passed a decree authorizing their return. But the Cardinal had taken his measures. Herwarth was on the spot with full powers from the Queen, with money to pay the troops what was due them, and with blank commissions. Orders were issued in the Queen's name to obey D'Erlach, whom a portion of the army joined the first night. The rest hesitated. But Turenne did not choose 'to repeat the disaster of Wallenstein.' He himself ordered his generals and their troops to bring back D'Erlach, and retired to Holland.

The Peace of Reuil brought Turenne back to Paris in the following month. He was very well received there, and Mazarin gratified him by reinstating by royal decree the House of Bouillon in its honors and prerogatives. But the two brothers remained in the party of the malcontents, and Turenne emphasized the fact by paying a visit to the Prince de Condé. When the latter, having made himself quite intolerable, was arrested on January 18, 1650, with Conti and Longueville, and lodged in the donjon of Vincennes, Turenne protested by leaving the Court and going to Stenay. Despite the advances that were made to him, despite the offer of the command of the Army of Flanders, he persisted in refusing to abandon Condé in his disgrace. The nobility did likewise, and this was the beginning of the Young Fronde.

To Stenay there came the Duchesse de Longueville, who, after she had tried in vain to rouse Normandy, had had to seek shelter on an English vessel, in order to escape into Holland. Turenne awaited her with an impatience in which some people chose to detect something more than political interest. It is undeniable that the Marshal displayed an affectionate devotion to Condé's sister, who, while jesting about his passion with La Moussaie, governor of the city, played upon it with the consummate skill of a finished coquette. In this sentimental intercourse Turenne was destined to be beaten. 'He was more deeply in love than he thought,' says Saint-Évremond, 'hiding from himself, so far as possible, a passion which he allowed others to see.' And if Turenne's rupture with the Court was not the work of the Duchesse de Longueville, at all events we must admit that her influence was not without effect upon his later conduct.

To make sure of the troops necessary for the liberation of the Princes, he concluded with the King of Spain, represented by the Count of Fuensaldagne, a treaty which the Duchesse de Longueville signed. He pledged himself to set the Princes free and to conclude a fair peace with the King of Spain. In exchange, he was promised two hundred thousand crowns to raise and maintain troops, five thousand Spanish soldiers, and garrisons for such places as should be occupied.

In our day, when one must not admit any sort of weakness in the face of the enemy; when no one is entitled, under penalty of being adjudged infamous, whatever his plight, to prefer individual plans of his own, however defensible they may be, if they depart from the line of conduct adopted by the government, which alone is responsible for the management of the war, Turenne's action would be a crime for which nothing could atone. For the sake of his own renown one would have preferred that he should have left the army, once for all, without trying to enlist it against the Court, and that afterward, being left without employment, he should have remained in his retirement at Stenay, through loyalty to the Princes. We have said above that such performances as his were the prevailing custom in those days, and if Turenne has been more severely reprobated than others, it is because his glory has always been so pure that we cannot bear to see it tarnished.

Did he not himself pass judgment upon his own action when, with his admirable frankness, he tells us that at the moment of his return to Paris, learning that many persons of quality proposed to come out to meet him, he arrived a day earlier than he was expected, in order to avoid 'honors which are assuredly of evil savor when one comes in company with Spaniards.'

Behold, then, Turenne entering Champagne at the head of Spanish troops, to deliver the Princes. He momentarily threatened Paris, and the Princes had to be removed for safety a long way from Vincennes. But it would seem that the qualms of conscience impaired Turenne's skill: before Rethel, where he fought desperately none the less, Du Plessis-Praslin gave him a thorough beating. Destiny did not choose that his arm should assist the foreigner to gain a foothold in France.

The year 1651 opened with a dramatic scene: Young and Old Frondes threw themselves in unison on Mazarin's back, and he hastened to Havre, set the Princes free, and retired to Cologne. Thus was performed the first of the tasks to which Turenne had pledged himself. To

perform the second, he attempted to conclude
peace between France and Spain, but the latter
was not over-anxious, for she had too much to
gain in the present state of confusion.

Turenne detected the Spaniards' bad faith;
he broke with them abruptly and wrote to the
Count of Fuensaldagne that, 'having done for
his part all that he had bound himself to do, he
was going to Paris.'

Condé, who had other plans, lavished upon
Turenne demonstrations of affection and gratitude. 'My obligations to you are so great that
I have no words in which to express my gratitude.
I fervently desire that you would give me an
opportunity to repay you.' But Turenne was
well aware that the public weal, of which every
one talks so much, has little weight in a man's
acts. Madame de Longueville's chain was
broken. Treason suited neither Turenne's disposition nor his heart. His clear-sighted honesty
showed him now where his duty lay. He resumed
his independence entirely. He tells how one
evening he went to see Condé and dined with
him, and adds: 'We used ordinarily to meet at
the hôtel de Longueville; but after that day M.
de Turenne chose never to go there again, for he
readily discovered, both from the intimations he
had received at Stenay and from what he saw at
Paris, that nothing was thought of there but

LOUIS II, PRINCE DE CONDÉ

private concerns and of making a fine external appearance which might deceive those who were not clear-sighted.'

As for Mazarin, he had never ceased to wish for Turenne's return. After Rethel, a rumor of the Marshal's death having gained currency, he had shown real distress, and had written very soon after to Le Tellier: 'Let me know if you think it well that, having an opportunity to open negotiations with M. de Turenne to get him back into the King's service, I should try it. For myself, I am convinced that nothing in the world would be more to our advantage.' And so, as soon as Turenne returned to Paris, the Cardinal settled the Bouillon business. On March 20, 1651, it was all finished: the Duchies of Evreux and Château-Thierry were given to the Duc de Bouillon, and the two brothers were confirmed in their titles of sovereign princes.

A few months later, the King was declared to have attained his majority. Thenceforth it was no longer possible to set up the Regent against the King. That fact would have decided Turenne's return if it had not already been accomplished. It was at this time that he married Charlotte de Caumont.[1] As a matter of dignity, he held aloof from public affairs, but important events soon put an end to his inaction.

[1] Granddaughter of the Duc de La Force.

Early in 1652, Condé revolted in his government of Guyenne, and entered into negotiations with Spain. Mazarin, returning from Germany, again found the Princes and the Parliament united against him. To hold the Princes in check, the Court had to go to Bruges, then to Poitiers. It was at the latter place that Turenne joined the Court; he was placed in command of one half of the royal army, of which Maréchal d'Hocquincourt commanded the other half. He set out to save the State when everybody thought it lost.

After halts at Saumur, Angers, and Tours, the King found the gates of Orléans closed against him and had to march along the Loire to Sully. The army of the Princes tried to carry the bridge at Jargeau in order to kidnap the King. Turenne, realizing the danger, had a barricade thrown up in the middle of the bridge, part of which was already in the enemy's hands; he defended it, sword in hand, with a handful of men, without ammunition, and in the face of the enemy's guns, thus giving reënforcements time to come up. The Court was able to take up its quarters in Gien.

But Condé rode from Guyenne at full speed and attacked D'Hocquincourt. His army was three times as large as the King's. Turenne, being summoned to the rescue, determined to fight, although his generals shivered at the bare thought of facing Monsieur le Prince with so small a force. But Turenne's talent made up for his weakness: he posted his infantry in the rear, in a defile, placed his guns in such a way as to work them to the best advantage, and put his cavalry in front to draw the enemy; then he waited. Mutterings began again about him; a number of officers wished to return to Gien, to defend the King more effectively. 'Turenne declared,' says a witness, 'that the King's arms would be disgraced if they fled from rebels'; and he added in a firm, loud voice, 'We must conquer or die here.' And every man remained in his place. Condé fell into the trap and led his troops into a narrow pass where they were mown down by the guns. He was beaten and returned to Paris.

From the windows of the castle of Gien the Court had been able to follow the battle; they were delivered from the very great danger that had threatened them, for if the Queen and Cardinal had fallen into the hands of their enemies, the former would have been consigned to a convent and Mazarin would have been in danger of the worst possible fate. When the Queen saw Turenne, she wept as she said to him, 'Monsieur le Maréchal, you have saved the State.'

The Court then went to Saint-Germain.

Turenne would have put on a bold front and pushed on to Paris, where the Princes were without troops. But Mazarin dared not. Turenne consoled himself by dealing a sharp blow at the army of the Princes at Étampes, where La Grande Mademoiselle[1] had chosen to divert herself with a review. His success would have been complete but for a mistaken maneuver of D'Hocquincourt, whom Mazarin decided to send to Flanders, leaving to Turenne the command of the whole army. Thereupon he took Étampes, where his regiment distinguished itself in an action, which, he tells us, 'was fought in sight of the whole army and was considered one of the greatest ever seen.' Then by the boldness and rapidity of his movements, he prevented the Duke of Lorraine from joining the Princes. Finally, at the beginning of July, came the battle of the Faubourg Saint-Antoine, when Condé, forced back against the walls of Paris which were defended by the militia of the city, with matches lighted, was lost when La Grande Mademoiselle ordered the gates opened and turned the guns of the Bastille on the King's troops.

But Paris, which cried, 'Death to the Mazarins!' at heart cared for nothing so much as a

[1] La Grande Mademoiselle was the title given to Anne-Marie-Louise d'Orléans, Duchesse de Montpensier, and sister of Louis XIII.

64

reconciliation with the Court. The latter was at Saint-Denis, threatened by a new peril, for twenty thousand Spaniards had entered Picardy. Mazarin would have had the King withdraw to Bourgogne and Lyon. Turenne instantly said that 'all was lost if they should decide to do that. He thought, on the contrary, that if the King should decide to remain on the River Oise and his army should march toward Compiègne, the whole Spanish army would not dare march on Paris for fear of leaving Flanders unprotected and the King's army between it and them; and that the only chance for the salvation of the State lay in remaining with the King between Paris and the Spanish army.' This wise and bold counsel won the day and the Spanish army withdrew into Flanders.

It was about this time that the Duc de Bouillon died. Turenne reached his side in time to close his eyes. He was deeply affected by his death, for he had always loved him devotedly even in his erratic moments. At this juncture, it was signified to the Court, that, if Mazarin would take himself off, all difficulties would be smoothed away; and the Cardinal, by agreement with Turenne, retired to Bouillon. Shortly after, the Queen, in the presence of the King alone, asked the Marshal if the King ought to return to Paris. The Marshal, who had changed his opinion, advised that that step should be taken without delay.

It was a propitious moment: Mazarin had departed, the King had already issued two decrees of amnesty, and the people were sick of the great nobles and their quarrels. So it was decided to take the risk, and on October 21 the King sent orders to Gaston d'Orléans and La Grande Mademoiselle to leave Paris. The latter obeyed, but Monsieur refused. The news arrived when the King and Queen were between Saint-Cloud and the Bois de Boulogne. There was a moment's excitement, the Queen stopped her carriage, ordered her women to alight, and requested Prince Thomas of Savoy, the Maréchal du Plessis, the Maréchal de Villeroi, and Turenne to come and give her their opinions. Turenne vigorously insisted that they carry out the decision they had made, because the people, if they should observe the slightest sign of weakness, would be quite capable of going over to the side of Monsieur. So they went on, dispatching a courier to Monsieur to notify him, that, if he did not obey, the King would teach him the respect due to his commands. Not so much was needed to bring poor Gaston to heel; he was very happy that they allowed him to pass the night at the Luxembourg and to take himself off the next afternoon at four.

THE FRONDE

At the barrier the King mounted and made his entry into Paris, acclaimed as a liberator wherever he passed. The Fronde was at an end, but Condé remained on the side of the enemies of France. Turenne, whose initiative, fearlessness, and political sagacity had retrieved a desperate situation, had redeemed his error. He joined his army at Senlis, for he had still to force the Spaniards to make peace.

Chapter III

TURENNE AGAINST CONDÉ

Mazarin returned to Paris early in February, 1653, to find himself confronted by extraordinary difficulties. The revolt was put down in the Capital, but it was still to be reckoned with in the provinces. As for the frontiers, they were all either violated or threatened — Gravelines, Dunkirk, and Mardyck were in the hands of the Spaniards; Rethel and Sainte-Menehould were lost. Mazarin had the courage, amid the most alarming internal troubles, to cling unshaken to his far-reaching external political plans.

To carry out these plans he had the good fortune to find in Turenne a most active and devoted coadjutor, and it is pleasant to observe how, from that time on, their mutual confidence increased and their collaboration broadened. The Cardinal kept Turenne thoroughly posted on all diplomatic questions, and 'the most secret concerns of the Court,' and promised him a predominant part in the Council. To attach him still more closely, he gave the youngest of his nieces, Marie-Anne Mancini, to the new Duc de Bouillon, then twenty-one years of age, in marriage.

68

The conflict about to be waged between France and Spain was really between Turenne and Condé. The former was to find that all his powers were none too great to deal with a situation that was made especially hazardous by the disproportion between the contending parties. The royal army, in fact, numbered only about twelve thousand men, while the Spaniards had more than thirty thousand in line. Moreover, the King's forces were poorly supplied with everything: they were short of munitions; they were meagerly provisioned and sometimes had to be content with the 'Cardinal's bread,' as they called slices of cabbage; they had no artillery teams and the horses from the King's stables were often used to drag the guns. In short, they had 'to do everything with nothing.'

Turenne opened the campaign by retaking Rethel; but the bulk of the Spanish forces entered France, and it became necessary to agree upon a general course of action. Important councils were held, at which the Minister and the marshals, in the King's presence, gave their opinion as to the plan to be adopted at so critical a juncture. A goodly number of officers advised stationing all the infantry in the frontier force and using the cavalry to harass the enemy and keep him from undertaking any siege works. The Cardinal was inclined to favor this plan, which would enable him to gain time without running the risk of a battle until he should be the stronger. Other officers, on the contrary, insisted that the army should be kept together, but that it should stay behind the Oise, to prevent the crossing of the river and thus protect Paris.

Turenne's view was altogether different: with an opponent like Monsieur le Prince, 'we must expect whatever bold and vigorous steps a man can take when his enemy divides his forces and leaves so many exposed points.' So that it was impossible to think of sending away the infantry if they did not hold the country. The army must keep together, but must not remain inactive behind a river, waiting for some one to come and attack it; on the contrary, it must make up for its weakness in numbers by its mobility and, 're-maining constantly within reach of the enemy, give him to understand that it would not always arrive twelve or fifteen hours behind him at any place he should attempt to invest.' They must always 'keep alongside the enemy, although it might be a little dangerous.' And he added: 'I insist upon this because, unquestionably, the decision to cross the river, to leave nothing in the fortresses, and to take up quarters near the enemy has made this incursion into France [of the Spanish army] utterly ineffectual; and often,

70

through being fearful of so many things, one adopts a course that turns out very ill; but when one has a good army, albeit the smaller one, and is very careful about one's camping-places, and about keeping watch on the enemy's movements, the battle is half won.'

That was a way of viewing operations which was not in vogue in that day. By suggesting and defending it, Turenne proved himself an innovator, for the plan was contrary to the usual routine. In putting it in practice, he displayed so much skill and prudence that he reaped the fruit of his audacity while he escaped the perils to which he might have exposed himself. This feature of his methods was to become accentuated as the years passed.

And so Turenne put his plan in execution, disconcerting the enemy by his mobility: sometimes he made a pretense of offering battle and stole away; again he seemed to leave at his enemy's mercy places with few means of defense, then blocked a siege of them by appearing unexpectedly. His activity was prodigious, and it aroused the especial admiration of the Duke of York (later James II of England), who hardly left his side, and who wrote: 'M. de Turenne was determined to look to everything himself; he reconnoitered in person, and at very close quarters, the places he proposed to besiege; he always selected the spot at which the trenches should be opened, and was present when it was done; he ordered the direction in which the digging should be done, and went there regularly every morning and evening — in the evening, to decide what should be done during the night, and in the morning, to see if his orders had been carried out. The general's diligence aroused all the officers in the army to intense application to their duty.' Thus we see that the Marshal was not content simply to issue orders, but overlooked their execution — an important part of a commander's business.

The year 1654 began with the King's coronation; then Mazarin decided that Stenay must be taken. The King went there, Fabert invested the place, and Turenne was covering the siege on the Champagne side, when he learned that Condé, neglecting to send aid to Stenay, had laid siege to Arras, which was defended by the Comte de Montjeu. 'If I take Arras, you will be the gainers,' he said to the Spaniards, 'and I in very much greater measure.' There was great commotion in the royal camp, for if Arras should fall, the position of France in Artois would be endangered. Condé had carried on the investment with such fierce speed that a part of the defending cavalry, which was on reconnaissance duty outside the walls, had no time to get in again.

Turenne arrived in hot haste and pitched his camp close at hand. His arrival revived the courage of the besieged. The Court insisted that he should attack the Spanish army at once. But he chose to wait until he was in sufficient force, and contrary to the opinions of those about him, he believed his troops to be capable of the requisite patience. 'It was not my belief,' say the Memoirs, 'that the French must be sent into action instantly, being convinced that they have as much patience as other troops when they are well led.' To questions of this sort which we asked one another often before the late war, the French soldier of 1914 replied by his admirable tenacity, and confirmed the opinion expressed nearly three centuries earlier by this consummate judge of men.

While waiting for the fall of Stenay to place troops at his disposal, Turenne made life a burden for the besieging army. He infused his own dash and vigor into the commanders of all the strong places in the region, and every day there were ambuscades, and cannon captured or destroyed, so that the Spaniards lost many men, wore themselves out in the business of being always on guard, and began to fall short of provisions. But he was himself face to face with the greatest difficulties. He was in need of everything, and his daily correspondence with Mazarin and Le Tellier demands officers, engineers, weapons, tools, bread, and grains.

At last Stenay fell and the royal army could be materially reënforced. But Turenne was not alone in the command. The old underhand intrigues, the remains of a mistrust often justified, still existed; theoretically Marshals d'Hocquincourt and de La Ferté had equal authority with him; that is to say, each of the three commanded his particular corps and took in turn the command of the whole force one day in three. It was, in fact, Turenne who held the guiding rein, but he was obliged to waste time in futile councils of war, in which he had at times to listen with a sober face to the most idiotic proposals. It became necessary that his supremacy should be established beyond dispute, so that he might be set free from such supernumeraries.

As soon as he felt that he was in sufficient force, Turenne determined upon a general attack; to prepare for it, he went out in person, with a few squadrons, to reconnoiter the enemy's line, 'who were making a deuce of a noise with their guns.' There were some losses, and old officers complained of being exposed to fire to no purpose — and it was the only time, the Duke of York remarks, that such a reproach was ever cast at the Marshal. And that eye-witness adds: 'Those gentlemen realized their mistake

CHARLES DE MOUCHY, MARQUIS D'HOCQUINCOURT

after the lines had been forced, since that was
the time when, exposing himself as much as the
others, he selected the spot at which the assault
should be made. And if he had not advanced
with the troops he had with him, the vanguard
of the enemy would not have retired as they did,
and he would not have been able to spy everything out so accurately.'

We do no better in these days when the claim
is made that the only way to reconnoiter an
enemy is to attack him. Turenne himself speaks
of this reconnaissance. 'That march,' he says,
'would have been a rash thing in front of Condé's
headquarters, but... I was familiar enough with
the Spanish service to know that before the
Archduke would hear of it and notify the Prince
de Condé and hold his council of war, I should
have returned to my camp.' Here we observe
the share that he allots in the preparation of his
enterprises to a profound study of the quality of
his adversaries.

His reconnaissance made, he decided upon a
night attack; 'he ordered the army to march on
a wide front, to attempt nothing in the way of
side attacks,' in order 'to avoid surprises'; and
as he knew that night marches are dangerous
things, and that it is easy to lose one's way, he
moved his camp (we should say, his base of
departure) nearer to the enemy's lines, in order

to avoid errors of direction. These are very nearly the same principles that obtain in our day in operations of this nature. The assault took place two hours before dawn on August 25. The troops knew every detail of the obstacles to be overcome, and they went at it.

D'Hocquincourt overwhelmed the Lorrainers, Turenne fell upon the Spaniards and Don Ferdinand de Salis, forced his entrenchments, and captured his camp; he supported La Ferté, who had fallen back at first, and the Spaniards were put to flight. But at dawn Condé intervened with his customary vigor and determination, and surprised a party of the royal troops who were engaged in looting the Spanish camp. La Ferté lost his head, left a hill from which he controlled the situation to go down to the rescue, and was defeated in a twinkling. Turenne then galloped to the abandoned hill with a few guns, which he turned upon Condé, who wavered under the fire and withdrew, saving what he could of his army.

The Spaniards lost four thousand men, sixty-three guns, and all their stores. The young King inspected the field of battle for a long time, gazing upon the extent of the disaster, and rejoicing that the losses had not been too great among his own troops, of whom only four hundred were *hors de combat*.

This victory created a great sensation outside of France as well as in Paris, where the fishers in troubled waters would have been happy to make their profit of a defeat. It raised to the highest notch the reputation of the Vicomte de Turenne.

But despite this serious setback the Spaniards would not consent to make peace. On the other hand, the King's armies were still so small that the campaign of 1655 was carried on in rather languid fashion. It was at this time that the Maréchal d'Hocquincourt, inspired by the Duchesse de Châtillon, of whom he was much enamored, entered into negotiations with the Spaniards. Turenne, being urged to march against him, replied that, if he should 'draw near with the army, that will drive M. d'Hocquincourt into some extreme step, and as long as it is possible to adjust the affair, we must do nothing to hasten his action.' He was anxious to save him from the consequences of a mistake like that that he himself had committed. His generosity delayed that gentleman's treason for a year.

In 1656 the campaign was slow in opening. Turenne laid siege to Valenciennes. Condé attacked the headquarters of La Ferté, who had had the presumption to destroy the entrenchments thrown up by Turenne's order, on the pretext that he did not need them. He was taken prisoner with four thousand of his men. From and after this disturbing incident, Turenne was delivered from the collaboration, with equal rights, of the other marshals. He avoided a more serious disaster by resolving, in opposition to the universal opinion, to show a firm front to the enemy. Then he took La Capelle, which saved the honor of the army but did not bring peace.

Indeed, the principal center of interest was no longer on the battlefields; the question was, which of the two equally powerless adversaries would be able to obtain the support of Great Britain. Spain and France were both doing their utmost to that end. Charles I had lost his head several years before, and England was now governed by Cromwell. He leaned at first toward Spain, which had been shrewd enough to recognize his government at once; he had found no less cordiality on the part of Condé, who had congratulated him because 'justice had been done to his deserts and his virtues.' As for Mazarin, as soon as 'he had seen through that man of incredible mental power, polished hypocrite as well as clever politician,' he was able to make up for lost time. The alliance took four years in the making, but in 1655 a commercial treaty was signed at Westminster. Mazarin regarded this first pact as of such importance that he had the ratification proclaimed in Paris by two heralds-at-arms attended by trumpeters, amid the roar of the guns of the Arsenal and the Bastille. It was not until March, 1657, that the Treaty of Paris was signed — a genuine alliance, offensive and defensive. By the terms of this treaty the two powers agreed to undertake at joint expense the conquest of Dunkirk and Gravelines, the English furnishing a contingent of six thousand soldiers to be paid by France. The first named of the two cities was to revert to England, the second to France; but if Gravelines should be taken first, France agreed to turn it over to her allies until Dunkirk should be placed in her hands. The agreement was signed for one year.

Cromwell was in great haste to get possession of Dunkirk, but divers circumstances made it impossible to give him that satisfaction as soon as he would have liked: the opposition of the Parliament, the financial embarrassment of Mazarin, the levying of new taxes, and, finally, the tardy arrival of the English troops, who did not land until late in May, were the chief ones. Then, the operations having begun by a diversion into the region of the Meuse, to draw the Spaniards out of Flanders, the English demanded the immediate execution of the plan agreed upon, alleging the great expense of the march and military outfitting of their expedition. So Turenne returned in haste to Flanders to prepare for operations in combination with the English forces. At Montreuil, where the general headquarters were already established, the King had just reviewed the first troops who landed; the fine set-up of these units made up of veterans, their discipline and their precision in the manual of arms, had called forth well-deserved praise from him.

Turenne's first operation was the capture of Saint-Venant. In this rapidly executed maneuver, all was nearly lost by reason of lack of money: the English troops, angry at not being paid, had vehemently demanded what was due them, and Turenne, to calm them, sacrificed his silver plate. He had it cut up and distributed in fragments, each marked with a fleur-de-lys. In his Memoirs he carefully abstains from mentioning this generous act, and we find no trace of it except in contemporary narratives and in a letter from Mazarin: 'You deserve high praise for your decision to use your plate in that emergency, and it is a result of your zeal in his service which the King bears in mind as he does many other proofs of it that you have given him.'

But the season was advancing and Cromwell grew more and more impatient. Mazarin, fearing to lose such an invaluable ally, persistently urged Turenne to attack one of the two seaports. 'I beg you, in this emergency,' he wrote to him in September, 'to venture something for love of me.'

Turenne, self-controlled as always, did not desire to risk any step that might turn out ill; but in order to give a proof of his spirit before going into winter quarters, he determined to take Mardyck, the possession of which would facilitate the eventual assault on Dunkirk. That fortress, under the vigorous assault of Mazarin's light horse and the King's musketeers, fell in two days.

If it was relatively easy to gain possession of it, it was vastly more difficult to hold it. In that bare shifting soil there is neither solid earth to camp on nor wood to burn; they were confronted 'with difficulties which cannot be put into words,' but which were familiar enough to those who had fought in Flanders in winter. So that, when the place was turned over to the English troops, they found themselves very uncomfortable there. M. de Baas, a brother of the famous D'Artagnan, having come there as a captain of musketeers, declared that they worked very slowly to strengthen the defenses of the place, and that 'some of them leave their work and use their shovels to dig up rabbits.' Observing this lack of interest, Turenne spoke of blowing up the fort and abandoning the town. But Cromwell declared that he should deem that step a breach of the alliance. Thereupon they set to work seriously on both sides; bread and other provisions, palisades and tools arrived in great quantities from England. Mazarin sent to the place Major-General de Clerville, at that time the best engineer in the army. He had occasion to employ as foreman M. de Vauban, a poor gentleman of Bourgogne, who was under twenty-five, but had already distinguished himself as an engineer in the assault on Montmédy, where he had received three wounds. Thanks to these measures, the winter passed without anything happening to Mardyck, but not without several alarms. The historic muse tells how Turenne was halted by one of them on his way to Paris.

Turenne, grand chef de guerre,
Qui prétendait avoir campos
Et se donner quelque repos,
Reprit allégrement la poste,
Pour se rendre près de ce post [Mardyck].
Mais, comme on l'a su depuis,
Que ce n'étaient que de faux bruits,
Je crois que nos guerriers alertes
Sans y faire ni gains ni pertes
(Qui deux à deux qui trois à trois)
Viendront faire à Paris les Rois.[1]

---

[1] Turenne, great war chief, who claimed to be taking a holiday, hurriedly took horse to return to Mardyck. But as we have

Meanwhile, the diplomatic controversy went on. To detach England from France, the Spanish offered Calais to Cromwell. But he would have risked too much by forming an alliance with the most bigoted Catholic in Europe, and he knew what rich stores of plunder Spain, if beaten at sea, would abandon to him. So he decided to renew the Treaty of Paris for a year, stipulating that Dunkirk should be invested between April 20 and May 10.

The time was very short. The difficulties in the way were tremendous, to say nothing of the anxiety caused Mazarin by the rebellion of D'Hocquincourt and the failure of a foolish attack of Maréchal d'Aumont on Ostend. The dykes had been opened and the flat country from the Aa to the Yser and the Dunes was transformed into a vast lake. But Turenne had planned his operations skillfully: arriving from the south, he skirted Bergues and joined hands, under the walls of Dunkirk, with Castelnau coming from the west. On May 25 the lines of investment drew closer. The next day the King arrived at Mardyck, the keys of which were handed to him by the English Ambassador. He wanted to remain on the field of operations; but the Cardi-

learned since that it was only a false alarm, I fancy that our watchful warriors, having made neither gains nor losses, will come by twos and threes to play the King at Paris.

nal, to get him out of the way, persuaded him to
go to receive Lord Fauconbridge, Cromwell's
son-in-law, who had come to see how things were
going. The meeting took place on June 10 at
Calais, and compliments and gifts were ex-
changed; the King gave a sword and received
two English horses.

Meanwhile, the trenches had been opened
before Dunkirk in the night of June 4–5. In the
following days, Turenne, while directing the
works, exposed himself so recklessly that Mazarin wrote to him: 'I implore you with the utmost earnestness not to try to wear yourself out
as you do by exposing yourself constantly more
than any one else; and reflect what a condition
we should be in if you should be wounded!' But
a noble example is never wasted, for a furious
sortie on the part of the besieged having put
the besiegers in a terrible position, the intrepid
gallantry of the officers of all ranks in hurling
themselves into the affray saved the day.

On the same day that the King was at Calais,
the Spaniards, whose camp was in the Dunes
near Furnes, were joined by D'Hocquincourt
and decided to march on Dunkirk to relieve the
city. On June 12, D'Hocquincourt was killed,
having to endure the shame which Turenne had
sought to spare him of falling in the Spanish
ranks. On the 13th, Turenne, whose forces were

now equal to the enemy's, decided to go out to
meet him instead of awaiting an attack from him.
He took possession of several high dunes to obtain the advantage of position, ordered an assault
on his opponent's entrenchments late at night, in
order to mislead him, and grasped the opportunity to reduce the numbers of the besiegers to
the profit of the assaulting forces. The troops
stole noiselessly into a ravine where Turenne
himself arranged their order of battle. 'The
Marshal, having nothing more to do,' writes
Bussy, 'wrapped himself in his cloak and lay
down on the sand, and I by his side. An hour
later some one came to wake him, bringing the
page of Humières, who had been taken riding
behind his master the day before and who had
escaped from the enemy's camp. The little fel-
low, who had plenty of common-sense, told the
Marshal that the enemy, having no suspicion of
him, had allowed him to wander all about the
camp; that they had no guns as yet nor the full
strength of their infantry; but that the report
among them was that they would arrive in two or
three days, and that they would then attack our
lines at once. The Marshal made him repeat
what he told him about the guns, saying to us
that, if he had not already decided to give battle,
this news would have determined him; then he
went back to bed.'

This is a very pretty picture, and Bussy adds: 'To rest only, for I have too high an opinion of him to believe that with a battle to be fought within six hours, he could have slept as peacefully as if he had nothing to do the next day.' It is our belief, on the contrary, that Turenne, having done all there was to do, having listened the second time to the news about the guns which so thoroughly confirmed the wisdom of his decision, slept soundly, and fought the battle no less well on that account.

On the next morning, June 14, there was to be seen 'on the faces of all our troops a cheerful expression that was of good omen for the success of the day,' the result of a well-planned affair, as we should say to-day. Turenne rode along in front of his forces, to assure himself that every one was at his post, and at five o'clock they advanced upon the foe. They marched in a line extending wholly across the terrain, about three hundred kilometers in width, from the sea to the entrance to the canal of Furnes; on their left was an English corps under Ambassador Lockhart, assisted by Major-General Morgan.

Condé learned through his cavalry of the advance of the French. He leaped on his horse to see with his own eyes what was toward, and returning at full speed to Don Juan's tent, he woke him and told him. As he went out, he met the Duke of Gloucester, who had never yet seen a battle. 'In half an hour,' said Condé, 'you will see how we shall lose one.' The Spanish army made its dispositions in great haste, the right wing, solidly planted on high ground, was commanded by Don Juan; the center, by the Duke of York, Turenne's friend, whom the treaties with Cromwell had driven into the opposite camp; the left, by the Prince de Condé.

The assault began at eight o'clock; the English fell on 'like wild beasts,' as one of their adversaries said later, and captured the dune. Castelnau supported them and completed the rout of Don Juan. The Spanish center held its ground no better. Condé, who surpassed himself in intrepidity, had reason to hope for a moment that he could force his way into the heart of the French line; but he had to abandon the struggle, and escaped with great difficulty. The battle lasted four hours. The defeat of the Spaniards was complete; they lost four thousand men of their supposedly invincible veteran infantry and four thousand 'natural' Spanish foot-soldiers. The French losses were slight, but Turenne had to grieve for the death of one of his best generals, Castelnau, who died at Calais as a result of wounds received after his marshal's bâton had been given him.

That same evening Turenne wrote to Mazarin:

'I am sending Pertuis to inform Your Excellency what has taken place. I am so tired that it is impossible for me to write the story.' Then he pays to every one who has 'done his best' the tribute of gratitude that is due him. And to his wife: 'The enemy came to us. They are beaten. God be praised! I have been a little tired all day. I bid you good-night and am going to bed.'

The Court celebrated enthusiastically the victory of the Dunes, which saved France and cast consternation and despair among the Spaniards. The King announced it to the country in these words: 'Our cousin the Maréchal de Turenne, by looking after everything and being present everywhere, has given innummerable proofs of his wonderful management as well as of his consummate experience, his signal valor, and his whole-hearted zeal for our service and for the grandeur of this realm.' While Mazarin wrote to him: 'I shall make no eloquent discourse to prove to you my joy in the victory you have won, for the thing speaks for itself.... The King and Queen cannot control themselves for delight, and Their Majesties have given you on this occasion all the praise that you justly deserve.'

There was much discussion at the time as to whether the Marshal made up his mind to attack before or after the Cardinal informed him that in his opinion it was what he should do.

Many contemporaries in their congratulatory addresses to the Cardinal ascribed to him alone the sole credit of the victory, while others ridiculed him and accused him of clothing himself with a military renown to which he had no claim. Such polemics appear at all times. They are altogether futile, for in the handling of those affairs which are a country's salvation there is glory enough for all — for the leader upon whom rests the weighty responsibility of when to fight and of conducting the battle, as well as for the minister, whose foresight and resolution have made success possible. And so Mazarin replied to the Intendant Talon, who must have gone a little too far in his sycophancy, 'I am very glad to learn from your letter that mine to M. de Turenne did its part in leading him to decide to give battle. Further than that, however, I claim no credit because all the glory is due to the Marshal, not only for the decision he arrived at, but for the splendid order of battle and the way in which he handled the attack on the enemy.'

In his 'Précis des Guerres du Maréchal de Turenne,' Napoleon wrote: 'Achilles was the son of a goddess and a mortal; that is the true image of war — the divine part is all that depends upon moral considerations: the character, the skill, the interest of your opponent, the ideas and the spirit of the soldier, who is strong and victorious, or weak and beaten, according as he himself thinks he is; the earthly part is the weapons, entrenchments, line of battle, everything connected with the disposition of material things.'

These operations about Arras and Dunkirk — and we have dwelt upon them for this reason — reveal to us a Turenne who leaves nothing to the hazard of 'everything connected with the disposition of material things,' but who also gives greater and greater consideration to moral factors. Therein he adheres to the divine part of the art of war.

Chapter IV

TURENNE MARÉCHAL-GÉNÉRAL:
TURENNE AT MAZARIN'S DEATH

During the night following the battle of the Dunes, Turenne remained with his troops, perhaps as a measure of prudence, but especially because he proposed to follow up his success and allow no respite to the defenders of Dunkirk, which it was necessary to take and turn over to Cromwell. The town fell on June 23. Two days later the King was on the road to Saint-Omer. 'He was dressed,' says La Mesnadière, 'very handsomely, his hat all covered with white and red feathers, and he rode an extremely beautiful and graceful white horse, appareled in gold-and-silver-embroidered trappings. Never in the opinion of the Court had his demeanor been so haughty and proud.' The besieged forces defiled before him; their commander, M. de Bassecourt, closed the march. He said to the King as he saluted him that it was his only consolation in so deplorable a disaster to place the town in the hands of so great a prince.

Louis XIV made his entry into Dunkirk and invited the English Ambassador to take possession, which he did the same evening, so that in less than a day Dunkirk belonged to the three most powerful kingdoms in Europe one after another. The place was not destined to remain long in foreign hands; and it fell to Turenne to take an active part in the negotiations which restored it to France.

At the end of the campaign all the fortresses in Flanders were in Turenne's possession. Napoleon criticized him for not taking advantage of his victory to march on Brussels. The Marshal replied, in anticipation, to this criticism: 'I have no doubt,' he wrote to Mazarin, 'that at this moment Brussels is in a state of terror, but I should simply allay it by taking a course which would have no useful results. To ravage the country and do no more than simply go and come away again would do more harm than good as matters stand.' We know to-day the military reasons which forced Turenne to make the wise decision to confine himself to consolidating his conquests, without extending them; we know the political reasons, too, and particularly the difficulties in which Mazarin had involved himself by handing over Dunkirk to the English. And so, at the risk of presuming to disagree with the 'Master,' we are tempted to share Turenne's opinion.

Spain, being exhausted, obtained a truce, and in June, on the Bidassoa, the negotiations began between Mazarin and Don Luis de Haro, which

finally resulted in the Treaty of the Pyrenees
and the marriage of Louis XIV. France restored
a certain number of places in Franche-Comté
and the Low Countries; she acquired definitively
Rousillon, Cerdagne, and Artois. The King
pardoned Condé. Lastly, and this was perhaps
what Mazarin had most at heart, Louis XIV
married the Infanta Maria Theresa, who re-
nounced her rights of succession to the Spanish
throne on condition that Philip IV should give
her a dowry of five hundred thousand crowns in
gold. The Cardinal had the best of reasons for
believing that the King of Spain would never be
in a condition to pay it.

Turenne made no haste to visit the Court in
order to enjoy his triumph. Indeed, important
considerations kept him at the head of his
troops. Before the conclusion of peace his army
had to be prepared for every contingency. Once
the treaty was signed, he had to attend to the
exchange of towns which its execution called
for. Finally, he had to disband a portion of the
army in conformity with very precise orders
from the King; but in the performance of this
delicate commission, he was careful to supply
the soldiers with means to live for some time,
and to ensure the officers opportunities to return
to the army or to take service abroad.

These various duties filled the end of that year and the early months of the next. Turenne joined the Court at Montpellier April 4, 1660. Then it was that he was made Maréchal-Général of the Camps and Armies of the King. He took the oath of office the same day. Did the King think of rewarding Turenne with the conditional offer of still greater rank? Many contemporaries declare that Louis XIV proposed to make him Constable if he would agree to change his religion. The Catholics entertained hopes of his conversion and made no secret of them; the historic muse, after recording the happy effect produced by Turenne's appointment, added:

> Mais si de ce grand capitaine
> La valeur devenait romaine,
> Beaucoup de gens à mon avis
> Seraient encore bien plus ravis.[1]

The same evening Turenne wrote to his wife: 'The King told me that it lay with me alone whether there should be something more,' which confirms the hints of the memoir-writers. The letter does not tell what his reply to the King was; but he was not made Constable, and we shall see under what circumstances his conversion took place eight years later. Saint-Simon opines that Mazarin was not over-anxious 'to

[1] But if this great captain's valor should become Roman, many people, in my opinion, would be even more overjoyed.

place a constable's sword in hands so skillful and so powerful.' We know that, if Turenne was not made Constable, it was because he did not care to hold the post at the cost of a base deed, and we love him the more for it.

The Court soon left Montpellier for the Spanish frontier, where the ceremonial of the King's marriage was in preparation. The new Maréchal-Général went along. On June 9 the marriage was celebrated. At the dinner that followed, Philip IV asked the Queen-Mother if Turenne was present, and when Anne of Austria pointed him out he said, simply, 'There's a man who has made me pass many sleepless nights.'

The young Queen's entry into Paris took place on August 22. Turenne, from the balcony of the hôtel de Beauvais, on rue Saint-Antoine, witnessed the passage of the procession with the Queen-Mother, the Dowager-Queen of England, the Duchesse de Chevreuse, and the Princess Palatine. Mazarin was there, too; but his state of health was so wretchedly bad that he had to be carried.

The Cardinal was, in truth, very ill, but he was to linger seven months more. We have seen how, in the later years, the confidence had grown constantly more perfect and the friendship closer between the two men who had raised France to the height of power that she had now reached.

Their mutual feelings revealed themselves in connection with the most private matters. For instance, in 1658, at the time of the death of the Duke of Modena, Mazarin, in a letter to Turenne, setting forth at length his grief and his reasons for bewailing the loss of that intimate friend and faithful ally, ended with these words: 'You will not take it amiss that I have written at length about a thing that touches me so deeply, believing as I do that I can speak of my sorrow to no one who will share it more heartily than you and will sympathize with me as a true friend, since you have no one who has more affection for you and is more truly your servant than I.'

Despite these demonstrations Turenne had need on several occasions to be reassured by the Cardinal concerning his intentions and his feelings. In particular, Condé's return to France did not leave him unperturbed, and Mazarin wrote to him on that subject: 'It seems to me that I have lived with you on such terms that you should have always the fullest confidence in me, since, aside from the knowledge I have of your merits and of the services you have rendered the State, I have extraordinary esteem and affection for you, of which, I give you my word, every one is fully convinced, and will be even more and more so since I shall never tire of serving you in all things which can assist in your gratification through my zeal and my influence. You can set your mind wholly at rest, and be sure that you will find me at this juncture as zealous and efficient in your service as I have had the good fortune to be on every occasion that has presented itself in the past.'

The Cardinal spoke the truth; it was shortly after this letter was written that Turenne was promoted to the rank of Maréchal-Général. So that he abandoned all suspicion. Thenceforth his letters were trustful and affectionate; in one of the last of them he said jestingly: 'In view of the courtesies I receive from every one, surely they don't now believe me to be at odds with Your Excellency.'

When he learned that Mazarin was near his end, he wanted to see him and made several attempts without success. He was so distressed about it that he wrote to the Cardinal's secretary, who called upon him to take him to the Château of Vincennes, where the burning of a part of the Louvre had compelled the Cardinal to take up his quarters. Mazarin received him affectionately and assured him that he had enjoined upon the King never to forget his great services, and that, knowing His Majesty's heart, he need have no fear on that subject; and that for his own part, he was truly glad to die his servant and his friend. Then he gave him a diamond worth a thousand pistoles, which he took from his finger, requesting him to keep it as a pledge of his affection. As the Marshal was leaving him, he said, reviving momentarily, that he hoped for God's mercy, but without fear, and added in Latin: 'If the world should fall in ruins, I should not tremble.' He died the next day, in the morning of March 9.

The Cardinal had been followed to Vincennes by many important personages, 'with their hopes and their fears,' and one can imagine the schemes of all sorts based upon his impending disappearance. Would he, like Richelieu, suggest to the King the person who should succeed him? Would he advise him rather to depend on the wisdom of a Council of State? Conjectures filled the air, and, as the question of individuals was not the last to be discussed, names were mentioned. Among those who were regarded as possible political successors of the Cardinal, as members of a council reduced in numbers, was the Vicomte de Turenne, together with Monsieur le Prince (Condé) and M. de Villeroi.

Turenne was, as a matter of fact, a very great person. It seemed as if his renown could hardly become greater, so near its zenith was it after the brilliant victory of the Dunes and the substantial results that had followed upon it, as well as the exceptional dignity that had just been conferred upon him.

Proud of his new post, he, a marshal of France for eighteen years, considered that it gave him a claim to higher command. The King's letters justified him in thinking so. His contemporaries were of like opinion. Says the historic muse:

> Turenne fut fait Maréchal-Général,
> Titre qui donne préséance
> Sur tous les maréchaux de France.[1]

Guy-Patin says that the old Maréchal d'Estrées died of chagrin at this appointment, and the Maréchal de la Meilleraye, for the same reason, thought of returning his bâton to the King. According to Saint-Simon, the King revived this rank in Turenne's favor, 'in order to put him over the heads of the marshals of France,' and he adds: 'He chose to wear no longer the insignia of a mere marshal, and he put aside the bâton with his coat of arms and the title of marshal, to resume that of Vicomte de Turenne.' The privileges that this rank carried with it were decidedly indefinite, so that serious difficulties arose in the sequel.

But Turenne did not owe his influential position solely to his personal worth and his military

[1] Turenne was made Maréchal-Général, a title which gives him precedence over all the marshals of France.

rank. To understand more clearly the place that he occupied in all the events of his time, it is important not to lose sight of the preponderant influence of the Bouillon family of which he had become the active head. The King had recognized the Duc de Bouillon and the Vicomte de Turenne as 'foreign princes'—a title which, by exception, both the older and younger sons enjoyed. Turenne never seemed to show any jealous pride for this rank, for which the dukes and peers could not forgive him because it gave him precedence over them, foreign princes holding an intermediate rank between Princes of the Blood and dukes and peers. They had bodyguards; they handed down their dignity to their descendants; they could remain covered in the King's presence at audiences of ambassadors; they enjoyed the privilege of being called 'Monseigneur' by the secretaries of state, and also that of the 'for' so-called — that is, in the quarters allotted to them on journeys, it was the quartermaster's duty to write in chalk, '*For* Monsieur so-and-so.' Saint-Simon, who tells us this detail, spares Turenne no sarcasm on the subject of his 'princery,' and describes all the petty quarrels that it caused.

Moreover, the Bouillon family, which was so thoroughly French in its far-away masculine sources, was related to numerous foreign princely families. The Elector of Brandenburg had married a daughter of Frederick Henry of Nassau, Turenne's uncle. At the period of which we are now writing, a niece of Turenne was the wife of the Duc d'Elbeuf, Charles III of the House of Lorraine; a nephew, the Comte d'Auvergne, was married to a Hohenzollern. The eldest of Turenne's sisters, Marie, was Duchesse de la Trémouille, and the first of her five children, the Prince de Tarente, had married the daughter of the Landgrave of Hesse-Cassel. The second of his sisters had become Comtesse de la Rochefoucauld; the third, Duchesse de Duras; the next, Marquise de la Moussaye. Charlotte, the youngest, who had inherited her mother's indomitable pride, was disgusted that three of her sisters should have 'contracted mésalliances, having married mere noblemen.' We already know her in the rôle of her brother's confidante. She never married.

Thus, by virtue of its alliances by marriage, the Bouillon family was European in the true sense of the word. The Marshal's foreign relationships enabled him to treat as one equal with another with the German princes. The Dutch knew that he was half of their race and that he had his first military training in their ranks. And lastly, Turenne was on very intimate terms with the Duke of York, who had fought under him, and he had friendly relations with his brother,

King Charles II, whom he had helped to replace on his throne.

It is easy to understand what solidity these relationships and these connections gave to his situation at Court, and also what an element of strength they represented in negotiations. Indeed, he had already played an important diplomatic rôle. To say nothing of German matters in which he had long been involved, the affairs of England had been the subject of a voluminous correspondence on his part with Mazarin and the King's representative in London. In 1660, he had sent across the Channel a gentleman 'who spoke good English,' to buy horses and carry his compliments to Monk,[1] to whom he sent word that, 'having long kept an eye on his conduct, he had conceived a particular esteem for his character.' The gentleman was very well received and brought back some interesting information.

After the Treaty of the Pyrenees, France was obliged to cease giving support openly to Portugal; but Turenne and Mazarin were agreed as to the danger of leaving Spain at liberty to crush or to absorb her. France, therefore, had entered

---

[1] George Monk held high rank in the Parliamentary Army under Cromwell, to whom, and to his son Richard, he remained faithful; but during the confusion after Richard Cromwell's abdication, he began to arrange for the restoration of Charles II, and met him at Dover on his return to England. He was created Duke of Albemarle immediately after the Restoration.

into a clandestine understanding with her former ally, in which Turenne played the principal part. It was he who concealed the secret envoy of Portugal, the Count de Source, in a house belonging to his nephew, and who caused his friend, the Count von Schomberg, to levy troops in France to be sent into Portugal. The Queen-Mother, being informed of these doings, was greatly displeased, and said to the Marshal one day: 'Do you know, Monsieur de Turenne, that I can look over Spain into Portugal?' Frémont d'Ablancourt claims that this 'frightened M. de Turenne more than the sight of the enemy had ever done.' The fright was of short duration, as we shall see.

The Marshal had also to concern himself actively with the support to be given to the Republic of Venice in its war with the Turks. It fell to him to discuss the organization of the expedition and to find a leader for it.

Finally, Turenne was at this period the moral leader of the Protestants, being by virtue of his rank the first Huguenot in France. If his brother's marriage and conversion had broken up the religious unity of the House of Bouillon, his own marriage to an ardent Calvinist had helped to keep him in the Protestant church, and to give confidence to his coreligionists. That is why he often acted as intermediary between them and

Mazarin. To be sure, the Protestant faction could no longer entertain any vast political vision, but it was numerous, wealthy, and included many men of worth, and the fact that he was regarded as its leader added still more to Turenne's prestige.

At Mazarin's death, then, he occupied a very great place in the State.

In that part of the Château of Vincennes where the Cardinal died, and in apartments near by, Anne of Austria, Louis XIV, and his nurse had been installed for several days. On the morning of March 9, when he awoke, the King called his nurse and asked her in a low tone not to wake his mother if the Cardinal was dead. As soon as he learned the fact, he dressed in haste, summoned the ministers, and forbade them to do anything thereafter, even issue a passport, without orders from him. Monsieur de Rouen, President of the Assembly of the Clergy of the kingdom, having asked him to whom he should address himself regarding questions which he had hitherto, by the King's orders, taken up with the Cardinal, 'To me, Monsieur l'Archevêque,' he replied. The Court was stupefied, the Queen smiled. But the King set to work, with what sentiments he himself has told us. 'I felt my spirit and my courage rise; I found myself an entirely different man; I discovered many things within me that I did not know were there, and I reproached myself gleefully for having remained so long in ignorance of them. It seemed to me then that I was really a King and born to be one. In short, I had a delightful feeling that it is difficult to express.'

The personal reign of Louis XIV had begun.

PART III
TURENNE AND LOUIS XIV

PART III
TURENNE AND LOUIS XIV

CHAPTER I

THE KING'S PERSONAL GOVERNMENT:
TURENNE'S PART IN MILITARY ORGANI-
ZATION AND IN POLITICAL AND DIPLO-
MATIC AFFAIRS

WHAT part was Turenne to play in this new order
of affairs, of which the courtiers sought to solve
the mystery? How was a man of such determined
character, occupying so exalted a position, to
adapt himself to the idea of a realm rejuvenated
and strengthened, and guided by a prince who
sought 'union in everything and everywhere'?

There is no better way than to follow him
through the early years of the personal government of Louis XIV — years of peace during
which he lived in almost daily contact with the
Court — to understand the part that he played
in political, military, and diplomatic affairs.

On the day following Mazarin's death, the
King assembled for the last time the Council of
the Great. The Princes, Dukes, and Ministers
of State, Condé, Turenne, Marshals Villeroi,

Gramont, and Plessis-Praslin — all were there. Louis XIV, after informing them that 'he had resolved to govern the State himself, dismissed them courteously, saying that, if he should find himself in need of their advice, he would have them called together.'

From that day forth the regular councils were held with only three permanent members whom the King had designated — Fouquet,[1] Le Tellier, and Lionne. There were extraordinary councils, too, to which he summoned certain persons, the selection depending upon the subjects to be discussed. Condé says that the King sent for him rather often, as well as for Turenne. Had Turenne given further pledges? He gives us no hint on this subject; at most he indicates, in certain letters to his wife, his wish not to leave the Court because of what may happen there of interest to him. We do not know whether he was disappointed, but we do know that he never showed any resentment.

[1] Nicolas Fouquet, Superintendent of the Finances, 1653–61, became very wealthy and powerful and almost overshadowed Mazarin. Louis XIV's suspicion of his ambition, supported by his vast wealth, was sedulously fed by Colbert. His fate was really sealed by the super-magnificence of his fête at Vaux in 1661. He was dismissed and charged with peculation; his trial lasted almost three years and its violation of all the forms of justice is still discussed by members of the French bar. He was in prison at Pignerol in 1665 and died there in 1680. He is one of the many persons who have been identified as 'the Man in the Iron Mask.'

Perhaps he hoped, as the whole Court did, that the young King would grow weary of the formidable task which he had set himself, and that the system adopted would not long endure. The arrest of Fouquet revived all these hopes. This affair of Fouquet, which was one of the great political events of the period, kept Paris in a ferment more than four years. At the end Turenne definitely took sides on it.

Although he had no liking for the Superintendent of Finances, who had often compelled him to pay his troops out of his own pocket, he espoused the cause of those who wished to save him from the capital penalty to which the King's indignation seemed likely to subject him. Was this done to oppose Colbert,[1] with whom he was never completely in accord? or from friendship for Lefèvre d'Ormesson, author of the reports which recommended only banishment? However that may be, the fact remains that Turenne dared to declare himself on the side of Fouquet's defenders; that is to say, in opposition to the King, who

[1] Jean-Baptiste Colbert began his career as private secretary to his uncle, Le Tellier, Secretary for War. When Mazarin was driven from Paris during the Fronde, Colbert acted as his spy and eventually became his confidant and was entrusted with matters of greatest importance. He began to undermine Fouquet before Mazarin's death, and after that event brought every means to bear to win the King's favor. By 1669, he was at the head of every department except that of war. His great scheme of financial and fiscal reform brought about the downfall of Fouquet.

sent word to him, 'in very strong language, not to meddle any more in that affair.' In fact, Fouquet's disappearance from the stage caused no change in the established order of things, and Colbert took his place.

Turenne had some opportunities to collaborate in the new Superintendent's policy of commercial and maritime expansion in the study of plans concerning San Domingo, Alhucemas, and Morocco.

But it was especially in the reorganization of the army, with Le Tellier and Louvois, and in the handling of important diplomatic matters, with Lionne, that Turenne's activity found a fertile field for its exercise.

Turenne had been Colonel-General of Cavalry since 1657, and he performed the duties of that office after the conclusion of peace. It was a very important post by reason of its prerogatives, amongst others the command of the Colonel-General's regiment which marched before all the others. It was still more important by reason of its functions: it was the Colonel-General who countersigned all orders relating to the cavalry, who worked directly with the King in the distribution of ranks and of such distinctions as the Order of Saint-Louis, and who signed all commissions, even those of members of the King's Household. As for the rank of Maréchal-Géné-

JEAN-BAPTISTE COLBERT

ral, in those days it was in the eyes of the Court only a striking manifestation of the royal favor — and that was much. But it was above all to his stainless character and his glorious past that Turenne owed his authority in military circles.

To that authority the Secretaries of State for War submitted. Le Tellier, who worked with Turenne for nearly twenty years, acknowledged his superiority. Mild of manner, modest, and ingratiating, he kept his eye on his goal; but with a natural distaste of anything that savored of pride, and 'in the business of life, he strewed only flowers.' He had, to be sure, in his work with the great military expert, some passing difficulties, but no lasting disagreement between them ever resulted.

Le Tellier continued to sign as Secretary until 1677, but in 1662 he obtained the King's permission for his son, Louvois, to try his hand at performing the duties of Secretary of State. This young man, who was a year younger than the King, was by nature self-conceited, dictatorial, and quick-tempered. He controlled himself on taking office, because he knew nothing and realized it; in fact, his father really filled the office for several years. So he made it his business to treat Turenne as a teacher from whom he had everything to learn; he made innumerable memoranda, solicited his advice, and his favor with the King.

But as soon as he felt assured of his influence with Louis XIV, whose pride and instinctive craving for conquest he inflamed, his tone changed. He became 'the greatest brute one can imagine.' He tried to encroach on the Marshal's authority and forgot himself so far that Turenne had to appeal to the King. For the moment Louvois resigned himself to the necessity of being only a pupil, and in the period preceding the War of Devolution, Turenne was in the front rank, carrying out a military task of the highest importance.

That task was, in effect, to provide Louis XIV with the proper instrument to carry out his policies. After the Treaty of the Pyrenees the army was reduced to a little more than fifty thousand men. The King's plans called for much larger forces, and those years of peace were a very active period of military reorganization.

It was necessary to reconstruct the cavalry, which was almost entirely disbanded. Turenne's first service was in the infantry, but he had learned to appreciate the work done by the cavalry, and his interest in that arm was already very keen before he became its Colonel-General. He devoted himself to enrolling desirable recruits, but he disagreed with the King on the principle of selection. The latter preferred the young gentlemen of the Court, who were able to

114

defray the necessary expense; that was the desire of the nobility, who were always eager for distinction, and was in the interest of the treasury, which was often empty; but those officers 'who go forth to death as if they were sure to come to life to-morrow,' in time of peace think of nothing but returning to their amusements. Turenne, on the other hand, wanted officers who came from more modest surroundings, and who were also more experienced and more devoted to their duties. The King's preference prevailed, but events proved that the Marshal was right, and they had perforce to come to the system proposed by him. Turenne did the cavalry another equally notable service by sanctioning the institution of brigadiers. Up to that time, when two regiments were brigaded together, the oldest colonel took over the command; but as his seniority was that of his regiment, it often resulted that a colonel younger in years and less experienced was placed over an older man who was of superior merit. This important reform was soon to be extended to the infantry.

This was the age of transition between small armies with a predominance of cavalry and armies of greater numbers in which the infantry was the most numerous arm. Condé had beaten the Spaniards at Rocroi with an army of twenty-two thousand men; Louis XIV was to march against

Holland thirty years later with a hundred and twenty thousand, 'three fourths of them infantry with siege and field artillery; this marked a new era in the military art,' wrote Napoleon. Turenne, who is supposed always to have preferred small armies, because they maneuver more easily and a general can know his troops better, seems not to have had any direct influence on this transformation. It came about, so to speak, by force of circumstances, the numbers increasing in proportion to the extent of the sovereign's projects, and the cavalry decreasing in importance as the infantry perfected its armament.

But in another field of effort, Turenne's activity and his influence manifested themselves most effectively in preparing troops for war. By means of frequent reviews he assured himself, either in the King's presence or acting in his stead and place, that the soldiers were well uniformed and properly equipped. The training of the troops was hurried on the more vigorously because of the belief that another war was near; in 1666 two corps were assembled near Compiègne, and for three days went through maneuvers intended to reproduce actual warfare. The King inspected one corps and Turenne the other; it was a veritable camp of instruction.

Again, Turenne looked to the maintenance of

strict discipline. We know of his goodness to those below him. He was determined that his soldiers should be paid regularly and well fed. He was tireless in indulgence for their pranks in camp when they had shown gallantry on the battlefield. He bestowed his favors on good officers and was always ready to take up their defense when luck went against them. 'Severe to himself,' writes Saint-Évremond, 'he reckoned all his misfortunes as blunders; indulgent to those who had fallen short, he treated their blunders as misfortunes.' But he would be obeyed and would not condone resistance to an order. 'I speak harshly to no one,' he said one day, 'but I will have your head off the instant that you refuse to obey me.'

Nothing can be better adapted to convey an appreciation of his manner, at once firm and kindly, than to follow the narrative of an officer who had to do with him directly for two or three moments of a very adventurous life. We refer to M. de Montbas, whom Turenne esteemed particularly because of his courage and his enterprising spirit. The Royal Cavalry, to which regiment he belonged, had lost its colonel. The King had appointed to replace him M. de Montpezat, an excellent officer, but a stranger to the regiment. Some men lost their heads, the officers of the Royal Cavalry refused to accept him, and even went so far as to exchange blows. Turenne came on the scene and sent for the three officers whom he knew to have most influence with their comrades: MM. de Verdelin, de Thieux, and de Montbas. After pointing out to them that they had blundered about the point of honor and that they were taking the risk of ruining their lives, he made a personal appeal to each of them. And this is what he said to Montbas, whose story we quote:

'"And you, Monsieur de Montbas, who are only a child — are you following the counsel and commands of your father? What are you going to do after you have disobeyed him? You will have no help from him, and having once been a captain of cavalry, you will carry a musket in some foreign country, and you will never dare to make yourself known again; and so you will die without ever rising any higher. Is this following in the steps of your father and brothers? You will bring dishonor on them and will be blamed by your whole family."

'Then he turned to us and spoke to all three: "Messieurs, all that I have just said is from my own heart because of the regret I should feel at your loss. But I will say to you from the King what he wishes: that I shall myself, if necessity forces me, compel Monsieur de Montpezat to be received at the head of the regiment, and after that, I shall be the one who will support him."

'At these astounding words, we stood speechless, especially Verdelin, who was at our head. M. de Turenne, noticing this, took him by the hand and said: "Look you, Monsieur de Verdelin, you have always a friend in me; don't destroy yourself." Verdelin told him that he would have preferred to die rather than acquiesce; but that as Monsieur de Turenne took that view of the thing, he had more respect for his orders and for the honor he did him, and that therefore he would give up the idea of being guided by his own feelings.'

So it was that order was restored in the Royal Cavalry.

Some years later, at the siege of Landrecies, Turenne fell in with this regiment again. In the course of a sortie of the besiegers, the infantry having been thrown back, Verdelin's company threw itself into the mêlée, regained the lost ground, and stood firm at the end of the trench until the infantry had reoccupied it. Turenne saw the maneuver; he went up to Verdelin and congratulated his company, saying that in all his life he had never seen a single company do so well. Then he had the wounded taken into one of his own tents, where they were cared for and fed at his expense. He gave one of his horses to a cornet who had lost his own, and, adds Montbas, 'he bade M. de Verdelin and myself come to supper with him, which we did, and throughout the meal he talked of nothing but our action.'

When peace had come again, Montbas, who was always of a trying temper, had some words with Montpezat, who disbanded his company and left him without employment. He went to Turenne, hoping to obtain a commission in Schomberg's force, then in Portugal. His former chief asked him to explain his whole trouble at length, then told him to come again on the morrow. Montbas arrived bright and early at Turenne's palace on the Saint-Louis. He found more than two hundred officers come to pay court to him at his morning reception, and went close to him to make sure of being seen, but could not obtain a word. In despair, he went out and stood by the carriage that was awaiting the Marshal. As Turenne was about to take his seat, he spied him.

'Get in, Montbas,' he said, to the general's stupefaction, and gave his coachman the address of Le Tellier, with whom he was then on cool terms.

But let us allow Montbas to speak.

'M. Le Tellier came out to receive M. de Turenne as he left his carriage and said:

'"Your Highness does me an honor which I

should never have expected; but I shall try here-
after by my very humble services to make myself
not unworthy of it."

'To which M. de Turenne replied, "Come in,
Monsieur, I want to talk with you."

'Then he turned his head and said to me,
"Come with us, Montbas." That order was
quickly obeyed on my part.

'When M. de Turenne was at the door of M.
Le Tellier's study, he looked about and said,
"Are you there, Montbas?" At the same moment he saw me behind him and said, "Come
in," so that there were only M. de Turenne,
M. Le Tellier, and myself in the study. Then M.
de Turenne said: "I did not come here, Monsieur,
to speak to you on behalf of this man who has
been broken; he may be in the wrong. I am not
going into those matters. But I have come to
say to you that he is not a man to lose; he has
been very valuable to me in the King's service in
all the campaigns in which he has served in the
armies under my command, and if you will speak
to His Majesty about him so much the better; if
not, I will take it upon myself to do it."

'To which M. Le Tellier replied: "He shall be
reinstated immediately"; and turning to me, he
added: "I give you my word."

'Then M. de Turenne turned to me again and
said: "My dear Montbas, this is all that I can do

in your behalf; you will be reinstated, that is enough; if the matter had not taken this course, I would have spoken to the King himself. If you had spoken to me before your trouble with Mont-pezat, I could have effected a genuine reconciliation between you, and you would not have come so near destruction as you have."'

This story, which depicts to the life Turenne in the exercise of his official duties under three so widely different circumstances, enables us to comprehend more clearly than any argument could why officers and common soldiers felt a genuine affection for him. Such a leader could lead them wherever he chose.

Furthermore, we must point out that during this period of his career, Turenne's name came to the fore in connection with certain important military projects. In 1664, during the struggle against the Turks, he came within an ace of becoming generalissimo of the Austrian and other foreign troops. The King was in favor of his appointment, being conscious that one of his subjects 'had deserved that all Europe should turn their eyes to him for so important a post.' The opposition of certain of the Emperor's ministers caused a different decision to be made.

Later, war having broken out between Holland and England, and France, while holding aloof from this conflict, having decided to take action against the Bishop of Münster, Turenne was deputed to prepare the expedition and to keep the King informed as to what happened. Then this war gave birth to a project which placed Turenne in command of all the Dutch troops. It was believed that his prestige would lead England to conclude peace, and the Prince of Orange to become a loyal servant of the King. Colbert had even harbored the thought that the House of Bouillon might one day replace the House of Nassau. The King became interested in this scheme, but Turenne declared that he had insurmountable reasons for refusing to take part in it; he had confided to Lionne that he would never consent to be put in the place of the Prince of Orange, the son of the man under whose affectionate guidance he had had his first military training. This reason was enough for his upright soul.

Diplomatic activity was no less intense than military preparations. In spite of the Treaty of the Pyrenees, the Spanish Low Countries continued to be the object for which Louis XIV hankered, and Spain was still the foe to be isolated. France was in alliance with both England and Holland, but she had found endless troubles in keeping the peace between those two rivals. In Germany, her action aimed at holding Austria in check by utilizing against her the rivalries amongst the German princes. This policy was a continuation of that of Richelieu and Mazarin. There was nothing new in it to Turenne, who found himself quite at home.

The King summoned him to meetings of his Council, asking for suggestions, and gave him lists of questions to answer, together with the duty of drawing up for his diplomatic agents secret instructions which complemented the official instructions. From 1664 on, he conversed with him frequently on foreign affairs with the concurrence of Lionne, with whom Turenne was on excellent terms and who realized fully the advantage to be derived from his experience and authority.

To understand the work carried out by the Marshal, we must follow him in the principal negotiations in which he took part.

We have seen how he played the chief rôle, although undivulged, in the support given to Portugal. In 1662, the marriage of the King of England to the Infanta Catherine of Braganza opened up new possibilities for this policy by permitting the passage through England of troops and supplies intended for Portugal. All this was not put through without vast complications. Schomberg, who was at odds with the Portuguese, wished to give up the command of the

troops. The Portuguese, considering what had
been done for them insufficient, threatened to become reconciled to Spain. Colbert, anxious not
to be kept out of the business, sent his cousin,
the Intendant Colbert du Terron, to supplant
Turenne's agents, Hasset and Frémont d'Ablancourt. And finally there was the talk about
'Portuguese marriages.' Louis XIV wanted to
arrange a marriage between Alfonso VI and a
French princess, and between his brother, Dom
Pedro, and a niece of Turenne, who never forgot
his family and to whom the King could refuse nothing. Turenne, being called in as adviser, ar-
biter, and defender of both marriages, displayed
truly extraordinary activity. The French military policy succeeded in ensuring Portugal's independence. As for the marriages, they were only
half successful: Alfonso VI married a daughter of
the Duc de Nemours; but Dom Pedro obstinately
declined the hand of Fébronie de La Tour d'Auvergne who married later a prince of the House
of Bavaria.

In England, as in Holland, his personal connections gave Turenne a considerable position.
England having taken offense at a treaty of commerce between France and Holland, Charles II
appealed directly to Turenne, while our Ambassador, D'Estrades, wrote to him: 'As the King
of England has the utmost confidence in you and

as I see proofs of this every day, it is most essential that you should write to him.' But Louis XIV considered that the ambassador had gone too far, and Lionne rebuked D'Estrades in these words: 'Whether or not it is for the King's interest, it is not fitting that any subject should enter into correspondence with a foreign king.' Things being brought to this point, the King took good care not to deprive himself of Turenne's services. For instance, in the affair of the flag, caused by an exaggerated pretension on the part of Louis XIV, Turenne intervened in the happiest way. He did not hesitate to write secretly to D'Estrades to counsel moderation, and added, 'This was the King's real meaning, although his dispatch was a little high in tone.' At almost the same time the redemption of Dunkirk was the subject of negotiations, the English demanding ten millions. It was Turenne to whom the Duke of York made it known that they would be content with five, at which price, thanks to his intervention, the bargain was concluded and Dunkirk was restored to France.

Lastly, when it came to the negotiating of a treaty of commerce between the two countries, the King addressed to Turenne a series of 'Questions relating to Commerce,' which the Marshal answered point by point, showing that, despite his relations with the English Court and his affection for Madame,[1] he was opposed to an agreement that he deemed disadvantageous.

Turenne took a very important part in the conclusion of a treaty of commerce with Holland. He entertained the ambassadors of the United Provinces at his house, and when the treaty was signed, the Grand Pensionary, Jan de Witt, expressed the gratitude of his associates and the States-General. Another important negotiation concerned the partition of the Spanish Low Countries after their conquest. To discuss this thorny business, D'Estrades was sent from London to Amsterdam. Turenne, being requested to give him his instructions, addressed to him a document in which he showed himself an accomplished diplomatist. In the first place, he informed the ambassador fully as to the general state of the public mind in Holland, the position of Mynheer de Witt, his incorruptibility, and as to the advantage to be gained because of his ability and popularity by supporting him temporarily, even to the detriment of the Prince of Orange. Then, passing from these necessary details to matters of broader import, Turenne advised the ambassador to 'be careful that the union

[1] Henrietta, daughter of Charles I of England, married Louis Duc d'Orléans (Monsieur), brother of Louis XIV, and was always known as Madame. She acted frequently as a go-between between Charles and Louis. She was on notoriously bad terms with her husband.

between England and Portugal does not incline
the Dutch to take steps in favor of the Spaniards.' He described the different parties in
Holland, and concluded with the opinion — of
which the near future was to prove the accuracy
— that 'we must always remove as far as possible
the jealousy that they may conceive of the King's
greatness.' It is difficult to display more tact,
more political acumen, more moderation, and
more entire detachment from all questions of
family.

In Germany, to prevent the Emperor from
giving aid to Spain, we had recourse to alliances
with the kings of Sweden and Denmark, with
whom Turenne was in correspondence. At the
same time he busied himself actively in assuring
France of the friendship of the Elector of Brandenburg, whom he tried to detach from the
Emperor. Turenne had agents of his own at
Berlin, one Bork and a Colonel Podevils, a Pom-
eranian now in the French service. At Paris he
took under his wing Blumenthal, the envoy of
the Great Elector; [1] he intervened between him
and Lionne when their relations became strained.
To the minister he insisted upon the wisdom of
the King's making sure of the Elector's assist-

[1] The Elector of Brandenburg, called 'the Great Elector,'
was Frederick William, the father of Frederick I, the first King
of Prussia.

ance, 'in case he should be attacked in the
bishoprics of Metz, Toul, and Verdun, and in
Alsace,' as well as upon the advantage he might
derive from it in withstanding an Austrian offensive on the Rhine. The treaty that was concluded in 1664, after long-drawn-out negotiations, was really the Marshal's work. One cannot
but be impressed by the perspicacity with which
he, first of all, realized the importance and di-
vined the future increase in power of the Electorate of Brandenburg, as well as by his accurate
sense of the rôle to be played by the Rhine in the
security of France, and by his assiduity in protecting it against the enterprises of the Germans.

At Rome, in 1662, the affair of the Corsican
Guard came to the surface. It began with a row
between the people of the Duc de Créqui, French
Ambassador, and the Pope's Corsican troops, and
became so embittered that Créqui left the Papal
States, while the King took Avignon and thought
of declaring war on the Pope. Turenne, who had
not been consulted in the beginning because of
his being a Protestant, was summoned when this
military project was suggested. He did not hesitate to take up the question from the beginning
and to speak words of wisdom, 'inspired not by
the religion he professed but by his loyalty to his
King.' His counsel of moderation prevailed and
resulted in a satisfactory arrangement.

In Spain, King Philip IV died in 1665 without issue by his first wife. According to the French claim, Maria Theresa, whose dowry had not been paid within the stipulated time, became his heir with respect to the Spanish Low Countries, where the law of Devolution was in force. In order to avail himself of this law, Louis XIV embarked upon a most complicated diplomatic game, in which Turenne had his part to play. He had been consulted by the King beforehand, and had given him 'an Opinion concerning what should be done in the three cases which the King of Spain's illness and the poor health of the Infante gave reason to anticipate': that is to say, the death of Philip, the death of both Philip and his son, and the death of the Infante only. After giving Louis XIV his views concerning the negotiations and preparations to be discussed, he concluded, extending his horizon as he always did: 'The King's armies and galleys will be, in all these eventualities, of fully as great service as the land armies, not only in regard to the King of Spain's possessions, but to Spain itself, to which access is so easy through Portugal, not to speak of the necessity of our having a fleet, the English and Dutch being so powerful on the sea.'

Turenne followed very closely the steps taken to induce Charles II to make peace with the Dutch. He strove also to bring Sweden and

Holland together. His sagacity is confirmed in his 'Reflections on the Use to be made of the Swedes,' in which he warned the King against the danger that France might incur of being drawn into intervention between their (the Swedes') enemies. These diverse negotiations resulted in 1667 in the Treaty of Breda, which reconciled England and Holland, and in an agreement with Sweden. Meanwhile, the King and the Elector of Cologne had concluded a treaty which Turenne drafted.

We might continue at great length with this branch of Turenne's activities, of which little is generally known, but we have said enough to show the importance of his diplomatic achievements. No question of essential importance was decided without his having part in it.

He had friends or personal representatives everywhere. He was in correspondence with all the leading men in Europe. He gave the King his opinion, by word of mouth, in the Council, but also in the form of reflections, reports, notes, or memoranda — documents of varying value, but each one of which bears the impress of his personality, while certain ones are noteworthy.

We have seen the qualities that he brought into the discussion of affairs: insistence upon exact information, discretion, prudence, exactitude, absolute independence of action in respect to his alliances and his foreign friendships, amplitude and continuity of aims, with a very marked turn for opportunism; and also, in the service of a youthful king, greedy of conquest, the moderation of a soldier long known to fame and no longer in pursuit of glory.

The personal government of Louis XIV did not, then, exclude Turenne from important affairs of state, for the King was already too wise to deprive himself of the valuable service that he could render. But at the same time — and this was where he differed from Mazarin — he had enough self-confidence to prevent Turenne, by rare but unmistakable snubs, from encroaching upon the authority which he proposed thenceforward to yield to nobody.

As for Turenne, he adapted himself to the new régime by 'serving,' without changing his character or abdicating his rank; and this adaptation, far from impairing his faculties, developed in amazing fashion their scope, their resourcefulness, and their originality.

Chapter II

TURENNE IN PRIVATE LIFE

Outside of the time that he devoted to affairs of state, what was Turenne's life during this period, which was unique in that it was passed wholly away from the army?

He appeared regularly at Court and took part in all the fêtes, ceremonials, and entertainments. He had a *pied-à-terre* at Versailles and paid his respects to the King every morning. It was not that the tastes of his younger days had changed; he had the same aversion to dressed-up courtiers and braggart soldiers. But he regarded it as his duty to defend the rights and privileges of the House of Bouillon, and, first and foremost, those to which his title of foreign prince entitled him.

For the same reason Turenne attended the King to Saint-Germain, Fontainebleau, and Chambord. At all these places, where the space was limited, one did not uphold one's prerogatives without a struggle, and our hero did not yield an inch in this matter. So simple in manner and sometimes so debonair, he went so far as to resort to violent measures 'if people did not give him steerage-way,' or if they did not show him the consideration that was his due. Sometimes

133

he played the fox, and Bussy tells how on one occasion, not daring to allow certain persons of quality who were visiting him to go away without escorting them to the door, 'he dodged this necessity by pretending to have business in his cabinet at about the time he thought they intended to go, and did not come out until he was told they were actually gone.'

In a word, he frequented the Court because it was his duty not to give up his precedence there. The portrait that Saint-Simon has drawn of him brings out clearly this contrast between his customary self-effacement and his instinctive pride of race. 'Singularly modest, even to affectation, as to his great qualities,' he writes; 'supremely haughty, sensitive, and on the alert as to his pretended rank as Prince, yet cloaking it all under a simplicity of attire, furniture, and carriages, whose somberness served as a background to the picture.' His 'simplicity' of attire was indeed proverbial and the balladist describes him as:

> Vêtu fort simplement d'un drap de Carcassonne,
> L'air assez négligé, le poil tout de guingois.[1]

At Court the King intimidated him — him who in the Council did not fear to hold his own against the most arbitrary sovereign France has ever known. He had no self-confidence amongst

[1] Clad very simply in Carcassonne cloth, with a careless air, and hair all rumpled.

the courtiers, of whose jealousy he was well aware, and whose sneers he dreaded. He was always a little awkward in manner there. He was reserved, distraught, taciturn; he kept his real self for his friends. His admirers regretted it; the rhyming chroniclers retained traces of this feeling. Says one of them:

> Moi qui t'ai vu le sabre en main,
> Plus fier que le Dieu Mars
> Faire trembler l'Empire,
> Est-ce là ce héros que tout l'été j'admire,
> Ou faut-il que l'hiver, dans le siècle où nous sommes,
> Les grands héros soient faits comme les autres hommes? [1]

Not at Versailles, then, must we observe Turenne in order to know him intimately, for he is not himself there, but among his own people.

Turenne owned at this time two houses in Paris. The larger one was on rue Saint-Louis du Marais, at the corner of the present rue de Turenne and rue Saint-Claude. His friends, Guénégaud and Boucherat, lived on the same street. What sort of life did he lead there?

The Bouillons were not wealthy. We have seen Turenne as a young colonel obliged to keep close watch on his expenditures. He had in-

[1] I who have seen thee, sword in hand, prouder than the god Mars, make the Empire tremble — is this the hero whom I admired all summer? Or can it be that in winter, in this age we live in, great heroes are made like other men?

herited from his family forty thousand livres a year, and had nothing of his own except Nègre-pelisse and three other properties, but his offices brought him a large income. Moreover, the King made him frequent gifts — on the occasion of his marriage, or to enable him, at the beginning of a campaign, 'to equip himself and attend to his duties,' or, again, as recompense at the end of a victorious war. But his contemporaries, who knew of his mode of life, altogether without display, his unselfishness, and his proverbial integrity, considered the royal beneficence quite out of proportion to the services rendered, and the balladist who was surprised by the great captain's modesty added:

> Que si de tes exploits la Cour fait peu de cas
>   Comme (à la honte de la France)
> On peut le présumer voyant ton indigence,
>   Je pardonne à ton embarras.
> L'État, plus d'une fois, aurait changé de face,
> S'il n'eut été sauvé par ta tête et ton bras,
> Et l'on ne voit pour toi recompense ni grace,
>   Tandis que l'on entasse
> Sur Colbert et Louvois qui ne le sauvent pas.[1]

Turenne died poor. After the payment of the

[1] If the Court makes little of your exploits, as (to the shame of France) one may presume from your poverty, I forgive your embarrassments. More than once the State would have changed its boundaries had it not been saved by your head and your arm, and we see neither reward nor special favors for you, whereas they are heaped upon Colbert and Louvois, who are not saving the State.

legacies, amounting to 193,000 livres, of which 90,000 were for the poor and 103,000 for his retainers and servants, there remained, after his debts were paid, only 250,000 livres. This is explained by the fact that he had not received pay in proportion to his deserts, and by his very great generosity. 'I have never been able to understand,' he said, 'what pleasure one can take in keeping strong boxes filled with gold and silver. If I had a considerable sum left at the end of the year, it would make me sick at my stomach as if I had to leave the table after over-eating.'

When he received foreign envoys or ambassadors in his house, he entertained them handsomely. One of them wrote that there were at Court only the Prince de Turenne and the Maréchal Duc de Gramont who had the art 'of attracting special attention by the splendid entertainment and cordial welcome which they extended to Frenchmen and strangers alike.'

In the army his simplicity was in strong contrast to the luxurious living of other commanders. Gonneville, who visited him at the siege of Arras, tells how on the first evening he was entertained by M. d'Humières, who had the supper served on silver plate, with the same delicacy as at Paris, and how, the next day, he ate at Turenne's table rabbit stew served on tin plates. But we remember the use to which he had put his silver plate.

Here are some other examples of his generosity. Dysentery having broken out in a certain camp, he borrowed from all the officers he met, in order to help the sick men at once, and told the lenders to go to his Intendant to reimburse them. When that functionary claimed that they wanted him to pay more than the sums lent, he suggested to the Marshal to give them receipts on account. 'No, no, pay whatever they ask,' he replied; 'it is not possible that any officer would ask for money that he had not lent unless he is in extreme need, and in that case it is all right to help him.' If he took an officer's worn-out mount in exchange for a horse from his own stable, he pretended to think that he was making a good bargain. If he gave another officer two of his horses because he had lost his own in battle, he would enjoin upon him not to tell anybody about it, 'because he hadn't enough to give to everybody.' We could go much further without exhausting the tale of his benefactions. Let us add only that, just before his death, he reëquipped at his own expense a whole English regiment and that it cost him fourteen thousand livres.

We can understand that, if he opened his purse thus to other people, he did not keep very much for himself. So that there was no ostentation of luxury in the management of his household. No memoir-writer describes his horses and carriages;

we have an occasional mention of the 'Magpie,' his mare, whose coat, with great splashes of white, his troops were accustomed to see always in the most exposed places. After all her adventures, she ended her days happily in the pastures of the monastery of Paray-le-Monial, where a fall from grace of the Duc de Bouillon, her master's nephew and heir, compelled him to spend his last days.

The personnel of his immediate *entourage* is well known to us. There was Duhan de Jaudren, his confidential secretary, who left France for Berlin after the Revocation of the Edict of Nantes, and whose son, noted for his gallantry at the siege of Stralsund, was afterward one of the teachers of Frederick the Great. There was another secretary, Hasset, whose work in Portugal we have already mentioned. There was Bois-guyot, a young nobleman in personal attendance on him, who was to make known at Paris all the details of his glorious death. And lastly, there was Pertuis, the commander of his bodyguard, whom we shall see at Saint-Denis, halberd on shoulder, mounting guard for the last time by his master's body.

All of them remained devoted to him to the end, for his kindness to his retainers was unbounded; a hundred instances of this are given, of which a few follow. One morning Turenne, who rose early, was enjoying the cool air at the window; one of his people, seeing a man there in a night-cap with his elbow on the rail, took him for a comrade and clapped him on the back. The Marshal turned about. 'Monseigneur,' cried the jester, on his knees, 'I thought it was Georges.' — 'But even if it were Georges,' said Turenne, 'you should not strike so hard.'

Another of his servants went to Colbert for employment as if at Turenne's instance, but without his knowledge. Colbert was quick to accede to his request. The Marshal thanked the Minister, then sent for the man, who, finding that he was detected, threw himself at his feet and begged for forgiveness. Turenne told him to rise, and said, 'If you had spoken to me about this I would have done for you all that you desire, but what grieves me in it all is that you should not have told me what induced you to leave me.' Then, learning that he had sought the new job because he had many children, Turenne ordered that there be given to him with his wages a considerable sum to help him maintain his family.

This same intimate kindness of heart he displayed toward all persons of humble condition. It is told of him that one day some players at bowls stopped him in the street to ask him to decide a doubtful point; he measured the distance with his cane and gave his decision, whereupon the loser overwhelmed him with insults. At the moment a group of officers passed and saluted him with the utmost respect. The gamester, terrified to find himself in such evil case, implored the clemency of the Marshal, who said simply, 'My friend, you were wrong in thinking that I wanted to cheat you.'

But with his equals he did not treat things in quite the same fashion, although even then he had his own way of teaching a lesson. One day the Maréchal de La Ferté met outside of the camp a soldier whom he recognized as one of Turenne's men, and he proceeded to beat him, solely for that reason. Turenne dismissed the soldier, who had come to him with a complaint, saying that he must have committed some terrible offense to have been beaten so, and it would be necessary to punish him severely according to military regulations. La Ferté understood and exclaimed: 'So this man will always be wise and I always an idiot!' There was, then, in all the acts of Turenne's life, the same contrast between an unexampled simplicity when only himself was involved and a haughty magnificence and sensitive pride when the rank that he had to maintain was in question.

His family occupied much of his attention. Charlotte de Caumont, Vicomtesse de Turenne, was a woman of rare worth by reason of her domestic virtues as well as her intelligence and culture; simple in her tastes, she had, like the Marshal, in the highest degree the sense of what was due to her noble birth and her rank. Judging by the Marshal's letters to her, it would seem that there was the fullest confidence between them to the very last, despite their divergence in the matter of religion. We shall have occasion to recur to the relations between them.

Although childless, he was, as the head of his family, responsible for others, for he had numerous nephews and nieces. While his niece d'Elbeuf, who was especially fond of him, gave him only pleasure, he had to deal harshly with the escapades of his niece de Bouillon. And it was with truly paternal solicitude that he detailed the domestic virtues of his niece Fébronie when it was proposed that she should marry a prince of Bavaria. 'My niece,' he wrote, 'will show the Elector all the respect and deference that she owes him. I am greatly mistaken if they are not content with her conduct, for she is very obliging, of a very sweet disposition, and has hardly been outside of her own home or a convent. One must not expect to find in her what might be expected in a maid brought up at the Court of France, for she knows nothing about festivities.'

In a word, he had to look after the settlement in life of both nephews and nieces. We have already seen and we shall see again that this was not always managed without difficulty.

Friendship held an important place in Turenne's life.

In his relations with his own sex he was looked upon as reserved and a little standoffish, for he accepted the bonds of friendship only with eyes open. Among statesmen he had no intimate friends except Hugues de Lionne.

As for men of the sword, we know that he was much attached to Fabert, who was a good deal older than he and who died in 1662. With Condé he was in unbroken relations of friendship, which, despite the rivalry which Louvois strove to keep alive, were such as they should have been between two men of great ability who, because they had fought side by side, and face to face, knew each other thoroughly and had the highest esteem for each other. Turenne seems not to have been on intimate terms with any of the marshals, and we know that there were generals with whom he did not see eye to eye — Bussy and Puységur, for instance; he blamed the former for his boastfulness, and he had to exert his authority over Puységur, 'the most intelligent and the most censorious of officers.' His interest was especially keen in the lesser nobility, to which most of his officers belonged, whom he loved because of their courage and devotion, and whom he was always ready to assist.

But these were not his really intimate friends; outside of a few great noblemen, we must look for them amongst the members of Parliament and the magistrates. The King knew it, and said to his mother: 'M. de Turenne loves me, but he has a higher regard for the lawyers.' In Paris, Turenne saw much of Lamoignon, First President of the Parliament, and tutor to the children of the Duc de Bouillon — a man of high character who was quick to resist the encroachments of the royal authority; Boucherat, who was to be the executor of the Marshal's will, and who became Chancellor of France, and Harlay, his son-in-law, and especially Lefèvre d'Ormesson, a councilor of the Parliament. The latter's journal reveals the intimacy of their relations: 'Having learned that M. de Turenne was in Paris, I went to see him at noon. I found him just sitting down at table with M. de Ruvigny. He begged me to stay, which I did.' But this journal reveals, too, the courage with which the Marshal upheld his friends who were in disgrace. The report made by D'Ormesson in the affair of Fouquet had greatly offended the King, who had denied him the succession to the seat in the Council of State held by his late father. Turenne interceded and tried to move him, but to no purpose, for it did not please Louis XIV to see the Parliamentarians protected by the great nobles so soon after the Fronde. Again, Turenne exerted his best efforts several times in favor of Guénégaud; his first intervention did not avail to save him from the Bastille; but when Guénégaud was released, two years later, Turenne went to the King, who begged him to say no more about it. 'But, Sire, he is my friend and neighbor,' the Marshal insisted. — 'Well, I grant your request because I can't seem to deny you anything.'

And last of all we love to find amongst Turenne's friends the name of La Fontaine, who was one of the loyal adherents of the House of Bouillon, and who seems to have been the only man of letters of his time with whom Turenne was in friendly intercourse. We read in one of the letters in verse that Turenne wrote to him:

> Vous souvient-il, Seigneur, que mot pour mot,
> ' Mes créanciers qui de dizains n'ont cure,
> Frère Lubin,' et mainte autre écriture
> Me fut par vous récitée en chemin? [1]

— which informs us that Turenne admired and even knew by heart the work of Clément Marot, and that that serious-minded man, whose favor-

[1] Do you remember, my lord, that 'Mes créanciers qui de dizains n'ont cure, Frère Lubin,' and many another line was recited by you, word for word, as we walked together?

ite subjects were history and religion, was not in
his hours of leisure afraid of a little play of the
imagination.

He was playful and sportive, too, in his intimate circle. He loved to tell stories, and when
he could read on his companions' faces that he
had told them before, he was the first to laugh at
himself. He had a pretty wit, too; when some
one in his presence criticized Colbert's severity to
Fouquet and praised Le Tellier's moderation,
Turenne remarked: 'In truth, I believe M. Colbert is more anxious that he should be hanged and
M. Le Tellier more afraid that he won't be.' He
did not turn his back on a good dinner or a game
of cards provided that it was with a party with
whom he felt at ease; for he took more pleasure
in friendship than in 'a thousand trifles which
make some people love life.'

He took pleasure, too, in the company of women. He was very reserved with them. 'The late
M. de Turenne,' says Choisy, 'was my mother's
best friend until one day, when she was old, she
said to him: "How does it happen that, having
passed our lives together, you being young and I
pretty, you have never said anything worse to
me than my name?"' But this reserve did not
keep him from appreciating their charm. Two
princesses were his loyal friends: Henrietta of
England, to whose family he was strongly at-

tached, and the Princess Palatine, whose intimate friend he never ceased to be. He was on very good terms with Madame de Sévigné, especially after Fouquet's trial, and often met Madame de La Fayette at Madame's; these two ladies called upon him at his house one day when he had an attack of gout. He knew Madame de Maintenon, too, whom he met after she became a member of the royal circle.

As for the Duchesse de Longueville, Turenne had long since escaped from her influence. At the time at which we have arrived, she was closing her stormy existence in penitence. As she always loved a fight, she was fighting for the Jansenists, dividing her time between Port Royal des Champs and the Carmelites. 'A strange creature,' says a contemporary; 'she had the faculty of making an uproar while she was seeking her peace with God, and of saving herself by the same bridge from hell and from the enemy.' It was in that convent of the Carmelites that she was destined to hear the eloquent voice of Mascaron deliver a panegyric of the man who had loved her, on the day, a few years later, when they laid there the heart that had once beat for her.

Once again, at sixty, the age 'at which,' says Madame de Sévigné, 'glory should be the wise man's only passion,' Turenne allowed himself to be stirred by the charm of a pretty face. He was unable to resist the curiosity of Madame de Coatquen, whose beauty and wit he greatly enjoyed, and revealed to her a proposed journey of Madame to London on a secret mission. Madame de Coatquen told her lover, the Chevalier de Lorraine, who told Monsieur, from whom the King was absolutely determined to conceal it. This is how Choisy tells of the result of the affair:

'"Have you said anything about it?" the King asked urgently.

'"I certainly have said nothing about your designs on Holland," M. de Turenne replied; "but I will tell your Majesty the whole story. I was afraid that Madame de Coatquen, who wanted to travel with the Court, would not be of the party; and in order that she might take measures betimes, I told her something about it, and that Madame would cross to England to see her brother the King; but I said nothing more." The King began to laugh and said, "So you are in love with Madame de Coatquen, are you, Monsieur?" — "No, Sire, not at all, but she is one of my best friends." — "Oh, well," said the King, "what's done is done, but don't tell her anything more, for, if you love her, I am sorry to tell you that she loves the Chevalier de Lorraine, to whom she repeats everything, and the Chevalier tells my brother all about it."'

Turenne was much ashamed of the incident, which went the rounds of the Court, and when any one chose to speak of it before him, he would ask jestingly, with his usual frankness, if some one would not put out the candles.

It was, probably, during this interval of peace that Turenne wrote his Memoirs. They include a narrative of events in which the Marshal took part, from 1643 to 1658. They come to an abrupt conclusion; doubtless he would have continued them with a description of his last campaign, had not death struck him down on the battlefield.

Although Turenne had received the highly classical education of his time and had never laid aside intellectual work, and although he spoke German very well, he wrote badly. His style is cold and awkward; his long and involved sentences are hard to understand at first reading. The perusal of the Memoirs, therefore, is a difficult task; but if the reader does not allow himself to be frightened off, he is well rewarded, for few books 'contain so much substance and pith'; sometimes, indeed, certain principles are set forth with luminous simplicity. The book had unusual success for a work of the sort; but its popularity did not begin to take shape until sixty years after Turenne's death. In the eighteenth century, eight editions of the Memoirs were published between 1725 and 1774, four of them in other countries. Four more were published in the nineteenth century. Their interest appeared so great to Napoleon that he annotated and added to them himself by his 'Précis des dernières campagnes de Turenne.'

Turenne wrote a great deal: his private and official correspondence, his various reports, memoranda, and instructions make up a considerable mass. The form was always the same — far from attractive; but the substance is always solid. We are a long way from having extracted from them everything of interest to the history of the age he lived in and to the solution of the military questions of his time.

Perhaps this is the place in which to speak of M. de Turenne's 'obscurity.' The Cardinal de Retz concludes his portrait of him with these words: 'There was always in everything he did, as well as in his speech, certain obscurities which come to the surface only on rare occasions, but which never appear except to his credit.' Saint-Évremond says, less mysteriously: 'Everything that M. de Turenne says, everything he writes, has something too much of hidden meaning for those who are not keen-sighted enough. One loses much by not understanding him plainly enough; and he loses no less by not making himself sufficiently clear to others.'

Was it dissimulation, as Retz may mean to give us to understand? Certainly not, we can say with confidence after all that we already know of his character. Is it, are we to think, at one and the same time, natural reserve and calculated reticence? Of a talent essentially practical, constructing his plans according to accurate measurement of space and time, and to his knowledge of the enemy and the lay of the land, and having a highly developed sense of possibilities, Turenne knew that a military commander, even though his purpose is to proceed to carry out the plan agreed upon, whatever may happen, is often obliged to adapt the execution of the plan to the difficulties or the favorable opportunities he may encounter. And it seems that Turenne was reluctant to reveal the whole detail of a project which he knew might be materially changed by circumstances; he issued only such orders as were called for by the situation at a given moment, sure of being able, when it should be necessary, to complete them in time, thanks to the planning which went on incessantly in his mind, at the call of events.

In the words of the Prince de Condé, after Turenne's death, 'I should have liked to talk with M. de Turenne's shade for two hours, so that I might carry on his plans,' one can but discern, above all, his regret that Turenne had disclosed to no one what lay at the root of his projects. And so, too, in the remark attributed to his troops when, after the fatal shot at Salzbach, his generals were hesitating as to what to do next, 'Let the Magpie go forward, she will lead us.'

This is why certain writers have considered that Turenne could see the details of the plan more clearly than the plan as a whole. We find the proof of the contrary in the work he left, as well as in the breadth of view of his military policy. But he revealed his thoughts only in fragments, saying in his orders only what was to be done at the moment when it could be done. The disadvantage of this system is that it requires the leader to be everywhere. This was possible for the leader of a small army fighting for a few hours. It would not be possible in our day.

Turenne's private life gives an impression of dignity, sincerity, modesty, loyalty, and generosity. None of these qualities is exceptional, but we rarely see them united, and when they are united in a man of such outstanding worth as his, they justify Condé's words: 'If I had to change my identity, I should like to be changed into M. de Turenne; he is the only man who could ever make me desire such a transmigration.'

CHAPTER III

THE WAR OF DEVOLUTION: LOUIS XIV AND LOUVOIS AT TURENNE'S SCHOOL

FOR Louis XIV this period of peace had been simply the eve of war. When he was ready, he sent his armies into Flanders, giving his ambassadors instructions to represent this movement, not as a hostile act, but as a mere entering into possession of what belonged to him.[1] So that when Spain tardily sought to open negotiations, the French plan of campaign was already in course of execution.

This plan, which was the work of Turenne, is distinguished by the scope of the initial strategic movement. From Hesdin to Mézières fifty thousand men were stationed, who could be concentrated in six days and who were divided into three corps. The main army was commanded by the King, who had Turenne with him. It was protected on the Flanders side by a

[1] The War of Devolution (1667–68) was so called because it was fought by Louis XIV in support of his claim that the sovereignty of the Low Countries *devolved* upon his wife, Maria Theresa, on the decease of her father, Philip IV of Spain, because of the nonpayment of the stipulated dowry, notwithstanding the renunciation of her rights of succession made at the time of her marriage.

153

corps commanded by Maréchal d'Aumont, and on the Luxemburg side by a corps commanded by Maréchal de Créqui.

The King, who was usually so reluctant to allow it to be believed that anything was done except by his order, expressed himself thus on the subject of the War of Devolution: 'In the steps I have taken, and in which I have followed M. de Turenne's advice as well as my own feelings, I have thought that his ability supported by my presence would suffice to bring them to a successful issue; so I have applied myself more earnestly to learning the profession of arms under him and to giving proofs of my courage, than to the particular carrying out of my plans.' It is futile, therefore, to appeal to the concordant testimony of contemporaries to prove that in that brief campaign it was really Turenne who was in charge of affairs. At the King's side he played a preponderant part, which indicates, if we can agree with the Court and adopt its language, the highest degree of his sovereign's favor.

When the King joined his army, Turenne had already taken certain towns. Flanders, ill prepared by its masters, had no army for defense, all its troops being employed to supply garrisons for the forts; whereas the French army, spurred on by the young King's inspiration and example, entered the campaign with intense warlike ardor.

Taking his military apprenticeship very seriously, Louis XIV took part in the councils of war, inspected fortifications, passed nights under canvas. He even exposed himself so recklessly in the trenches that Turenne told him that 'he himself would retire if His Majesty did not take better care of himself.'

The first siege in which he took part was that of Tournai. He arrived on June 21, with Turenne, before the town, which, under a very intense bombardment, fell on the 25th. The King made his entry in great pomp. Then the army took Douai while Maréchal d'Aumont captured Bergues, Furnes, and Courtrai.

Thereupon Louis XIV, wishful to display to his new subjects the magnificence of the Court of France, went to Compiègne to fetch the Queen to the army.

After his return they laid siege to Lille. The undertaking was more difficult than the preceding ones because the Spaniards were beginning to pull themselves together and had under Marsin a force of six thousand men who held the country, while the French forces were reduced by the garrisons of the conquered towns. So that Turenne was obliged to call upon Créqui, to entrust Vauban with the siege work, and to do some tough fighting. Lille was taken late in August. The King left the army after this triumph, which aroused great enthusiasm. Then, Marsin's force having been defeated in a spirited conflict which cost him five hundred in killed, fifteen hundred prisoners, and eighteen standards, and Alost also having fallen, they went into winter quarters.

The campaign was at an end; for Turenne, who had conceived it and conducted it, it was a complete success, since the King had gone from victory to victory. Did Turenne derive unalloyed satisfaction from it?

In the first place, it is allowable to doubt it from a military standpoint. The war he had fought, carried on in a monotonous succession of sieges without any of those maneuvers in which he delighted, had, to be sure, given the young King his baptism of victory, but the Marshal was bound to reflect that it had added nothing to his own glory. Doubtless he could do no more in any war against an adversary who had only fortresses and no army, as also under a prince who must by no means be exposed to any danger of defeat. But despite the honor, of which he assuredly was keenly sensible, of being the King's teacher in the art of war, and his satisfaction in consolidating the credit of a Bouillon, he must have looked forward to a time when, set free from that honorific preceptorate, he would be able to wage war as he understood the term, and as he had occasion to define it to

Condé when he questioned him concerning the general conduct of war:

'Undertake few sieges and fight plenty of battles. When you are surely master of the country, villages are worth as much as forts. But men consider their honor at stake in the difficult capture of a strongly fortified town much more than in devising a method of easy conquest of a whole province. If the King of Spain had spent on troops what it has cost him in men and money to lay sieges and fortify towns, he would be to-day the greatest of all kings.'

On the other hand, just by reason of the favor he enjoyed, he encountered serious obstacles of which it may not be amiss to mention the chief ones.

The first subject of divergent opinion between him and the King's circle arose from the luxurious way in which the great nobles chose to live while with the army. The example came from an exalted source. 'All that you have heard of the magnificence of Solomon,' writes Bussy, 'and of the pomp of the King of Persia, is not to be compared to the luxury that attends the King on his journeys. One sees nothing in the streets except plumes and gold-lace coats in chariots, and mules in gorgeous harnesses, prancing horses and trappings of fine gold.' Indeed, there were thirty-eight horses, they say, in the outfits of courtiers, regular officers, or volunteers. People went to see a siege as to a play, not afraid, to do them justice, to go out to be killed as bravely as anybody.

Turenne strove hard to reform these customs, and he induced the King to order that no one should join the army with more than two servants. This alone was enough to cause much discontent.

Other difficulties arose in connection with the command. Maréchal d'Aumont claimed that the Maréchal-Général had no right to give him orders; but this time the trouble soon subsided. Créqui thought that the mission entrusted to him was unworthy of him. As for Monsieur (the King's brother), who should theoretically have taken over the command in the King's absence, he made no concealment of his anger with Turenne, who was compelled to reduce the number of his guards from five hundred to one hundred.

However, the whole Court attended upon the King and with it some of the marshals, as Plessis-Praslin, Gramont, and Villeroi, who were Turenne's seniors. Every one who had nothing else to do passed his time in criticizing the doings, actual or alleged, of whoever enjoyed the royal favor.

With the Ministers things did not go too

smoothly. The peace-loving and economical Colbert wanted an army that cost little and believed in having the upkeep of the troops paid for by wealthy noblemen. Turenne persisted in his demand for experienced and disciplined officers. As for Louvois, he, like the King, had attended Turenne's school; it was essential that military operations should not suffer from a lack of organization, for his influence depended upon it. His cause, therefore, was bound up with the Marshal's, to whom he was deferential and complaisant. 'But Louvois,' said Rousset, 'is not the real man; he is a bound and cowed Louvois gnawing at his bonds.' The real Louvois began to reveal himself in the correspondence he carried on with certain of Turenne's subordinates, of whom he was trying to form a little clique of his own, and especially with intendants, whom he instructed to keep him fully posted concerning the operations, in addition to their regular duties. And now we can anticipate the difficulties with which Turenne was confronted in the ensuing campaign.

The stay of operations led to a revival of diplomatic activity. Holland, with whose threatening attitude the King was concerned, had, from the entry of the French troops into Flanders, expressed her surprise that she had neither been consulted nor even advised of it. And so, when she offered to mediate, Louis XIV hesitated between the advice of Colbert and that of Louvois, who urged Turenne to support him, lest Colbert should carry his point. The King quickly decided to continue the war, for as he wrote on September 20 to Turenne, 'I am revolving in my brain plans which I do not think impossible, and they seem to me excellent!'

He sought all the more earnestly an understanding with the Dutch on the question, already of long standing, of the position of the Spanish Low Countries. He asked Turenne to let him know his opinion about it. 'His Majesty is well aware,' the Marshal replied with his customary outspokenness, 'that my advice has always been to let the Dutch see that the King places a limit on his conquests.' These negotiations came to nothing.

At the same time the King was seeking a *rapprochement* with England. It was a delicate business and Lionne called Turenne to his assistance. 'I want you to be here to back me up, as I am sure that you will agree with me.' The Marshal pointed out the tactics to be followed, insisting that 'we must always have it in mind to let it be understood that a rupture between the King and the Dutch is almost unquestionable if the war lasts.' Louis XIV then already

MICHEL LE TELLIER, MARQUIS DE LOUVOIS

had in mind war between France and Holland. It is well not to forget this, in order to comprehend Turenne's feelings at the time of the Peace of Aix-la-Chapelle.

Thus Turenne continued to play a leading part. This will give us an idea of the delight with which those who were envious of his favor even more than of his renown heard the news that the Prince de Condé had been put at the head of the army. They chose to see therein the certain decline of Turenne's influence, and they took delight in remarking on the painful surprise that he must have felt. We know, on the contrary, that Turenne knew all about the King's plans with respect to Condé, and that it was, as Louvois wrote to him, a decision of which he had long been aware. Moreover, Condé, as Governor of the Province of Bourgogne, was better situated than any one else to prepare secretly the operations against Franche-Comté. It was so that Turenne regarded it, and there is nothing to justify the assertion that he was displeased to see his old rival again given a high command. Louvois alone rejoiced to note that during the Franche-Comté campaign Turenne remained idle.

Every one knows the story of that campaign. The King left his capital February 2, 1658, and returned on the 24th of the same month, having in a few days conquered, without special glory, the province he coveted. Bad news awaited him at Paris.

Holland, England, and Sweden had formed the Triple Alliance to force France to make peace. At the news the King felt the keenest resentment. His pride brooked ill the idea of little Holland placing herself athwart his schemes, and his sense of honor led him to regard this action as a felonious one. But he restrained himself and weighed coolly the counsels that were given him. Condé, Turenne, and Louvois were for war, because they considered that there is an advantage in surprising a foe who is unprepared; whereas Colbert and Lionne inclined toward peace by reason of the state of the finances and the perplexities of a very complicated external situation. The advice of these latter prevailed.

The treaty was signed at Aix-la-Chapelle on May 2. Louis XIV showed great moderation, for he restored Franche-Comté. But the resultant frontier was a chancy thing, the French and Spanish fortresses were so intermingled there. And the question of the Queen's rights, really the sole subject of the war, was not solved at all.

To Turenne, the news of this treaty was 'a knock-down blow' — that is what Le Tellier told his son as they were jesting about the frankness with which the Marshal had expressed his opinion. Like the Marshal, public opinion was ill-content; it felt that a chance had been thrown away. Many historians have since expressed the same feeling about this short campaign, which gained no advantage and increased the number and strength of the King's enemies. Turenne's knock-down blow had no personal significance, but simply expressed his feeling concerning French interests.

As a matter of fact, what was signed at Aix-la-Chapelle was an armistice rather than a real peace. The Spanish Ambassador wrote that it would soon be the turn of the United Provinces; and D'Estrades declared too freely his belief that his master 'would pay the cheese merchants with interest for the duplicity of their actions.'

The four ensuing years, down to the beginning of the war with Holland, were employed by the King in collecting as many aces as possible in his hand by isolating the Low Countries and increasing his military strength to its maximum.

Turenne had an important part in all the negotiations. He drafted instructions for Colbert de Croissy, Ambassador at London, for he had the full confidence of King Charles II, who wrote to his sister: 'I am very glad that M. de Turenne is so friendly with you, for I am very fond of him; I am sure that he will be most useful in this negotiation.' But when Madame wrote from England that her brother wished to see Turenne, to discuss the military measures essential for his speedy opening of the campaign against the Dutch, Louis XIV refused. Once more he barred the way to that one of his subjects who might become too prominent.

This series of negotiations included the journey of the brother of the Elector of Bavaria to Paris, which ended in the marriage of that prince to Turenne's niece.

However, we find Turenne still clinging to his ideas as to the future rôle to be played by the Brandenburger. Despite the alliance that united the Bouillons with the Bavarian family, he considered it 'much more important to have the Elector of Brandenburg for an ally than him of Bavaria.' But if his judgment was accurate in his forecast of the future development of Prussia, he was less far-sighted in trusting the Brandenburger's word, for in 1672 he became an ally of the Dutch.

Although no essential negotiations were carried on during this period without Turenne's being mixed up in them, he was no longer indispensable as before.

The King had finished his apprenticeship, and

now he was reigning, holding the scales even between his advisers.

Before we come to the part played by Turenne in the struggle that was about to begin, we must pause at the momentous step that he had just taken, his conversion to Catholicism.

CHAPTER IV

THE CONVERSION

TURENNE became converted in 1668. Everybody
was surprised by the news. But despite its ap-
parent suddenness, no decision was ever more
deliberately made. It was the work of a mind
which liked to build only on solid ground, of a
conscience hard to satisfy, and of a spirit which
sought its path in the most lofty regions. Choisy
tells us how 'Turenne being in company one
day with Van Beuning, the Dutch Ambassador,
after they had talked a while about religion, Van
Beuning admitted that, if he were fully persuaded that there could be but one right religion,
he should choose the Catholic, but he believed
that one could go to Heaven by different roads. —
"If I believed as you do," Turenne replied, "I
should very soon be a Catholic; should not one
always take the safest path?"' Eager for the
truth, but also a realist who would not be content with words — such he continued to be from
the day of his first doubts to that of his abjuration.

Turenne had grown to maturity in a Protestant family. His father had no great influence on
the religious training of his son, who was quite

young when he died. We cannot say the same of his mother, of whose Protestant fervor we are already aware. Three of his sisters shared to the end their mother's ardor: Mademoiselle de Bouillon, of whom Racine wrote that 'she would rather see her brother on the scaffold than have him turn Catholic'; the Duchesse de la Trémouille, who was called the 'Pope of the Huguenots'; and the Duchesse de Duras, who died two years after the Revocation of the Edict of Nantes, as a result, it was said, of the grief that that measure caused her.

The Duchesse de Bouillon had entrusted the instruction of her younger son to Tilenus, a learned Calvinistic minister who was indebted to his renown for being called 'of Germany.' Eager in controversy, but of changing mood, he took up with several sects in succession and defended them all with equal heat, so that they could not keep him at Sedan. In his school Turenne learned to abhor that sort of quarrel.

In his youth he was a good Protestant; indeed, he tells his own people how one Friday he ate meat privily in his bedroom. A few years after he entered the King's service, he refused the hand of a niece of Richelieu, giving as an excuse the difference in religion. In 1642 and 1643 he often had occasion to meet under the roof of the Duc de Vendôme the Bishop of Soissons, who, impressed by his sincerity and his interest, hoped for a moment to lead him into the Catholic fold; but his hour had not come. And yet he knew — we have already said it and Brienne confirms it — that 'the late King had often declared that he would give him neither a marshal's bâton nor even the government of a province so long as he should profess the so-called Reformed religion, and that the Queen was aware of it.' His brother's conversion did not make him waver. In vain did Mazarin offer him the hand of his niece, Hortense Mancini; he married Charlotte de Caumont, granddaughter of the Duc de La Force — a union that strengthened the ties which bound him to Protestantism. In his last will the Duc de Bouillon had prayed God 'to make himself known to the Vicomte de Turenne'; but he remained immovable, immune to the temptations of ambition, unyielding to his brother's influence.

But it was in the years following the death of the Duc de Bouillon that his mind and his conscience began to work. From Retz we learn that even before his marriage Turenne was present with the Maréchal de La Force at conversations on religious subjects at the house of Madame de Rambure, a puritanical and learned Huguenot. So that we are not surprised to learn from his letters to Madame de Turenne with what sort of reading he fed his mind while fighting the Spaniards.

In 1656, in the trenches before Marle, he read the memoirs of the Protestant minister du Plessis-Mornay, whose spirit of toleration and desire to see the two churches reunited he approved. Before Furnes, a few days after the victory of the Dunes, he refers to them again: 'I turn very often to the books of M. du Plessis and see in his divided opinion on the subject of those of the religion the most reconciling thing that it is possible to imagine at this time.' A little later, he takes a different tone: it is certain 'that I discover a wonderful blessing of God upon all that I undertake. I am sometimes a little the better man for it; often, too, when things go none too well, I say sincerely how matters are with me.'

The following year it was another book, a Catholic one this time, which gave him food for reflection — Fra Paolo Sarpi's on the Council of Trent. Turenne remarks, without indignation, that the author enjoins upon us to do honor and reverence to images. He finds no less natural the homage that Catholics pay to the Cross. 'I see some,' he says, 'who pull their hats over their eyes when they pass it; for my part, I much prefer to take mine off.'

In 1660 his progress became more marked. 'I

have read a collection made at Port-Royal of everything that the Fathers of the early centuries said about the Eucharist. If it is not true, it can be contradicted, but I assure you that it is not what we say of it.' This book was the work of Nicole, and the part that interested Turenne so deeply was entitled 'The Tradition of the Church concerning the Eucharist.'

These letters show in what degree Turenne's mind was already intent upon the religious problem, and his desire to lead the life of a good man. They show us how he passed from Protestant writings to the study of Catholic books. Those that he selected put him at once in touch with the essential question which then divided the two camps — belief in the Eucharist as Catholic doctrine teaches it.

On the other hand, Turenne, who was always well posted on what happened in England, observed that 'every man, Bible in hand, sets forth in the pulpit whatever he pleases,' and that 'by overmuch independence of mind, but with common-sense and, it may be, devotion, the English have distorted Religion; each person who reads the Word of God starts a sect of his own.' Turenne grieves to find among his French co-religionists that independence of mind which borders on confusion of thinking and the violent controversies that spring from it. In the course of a journey that he took with the King, he wrote, apropos of the ministers of Montauban: 'One becomes surer by experience that the independence of ministers cannot be reconciled with established order.'

These discussions followed the Marshal into his own home. His palace was one of the active centers of Protestantism, for Madame de Turenne was a Protestant who adored disputations, to whom the most distinguished pastors dedicated collections of sermons. Madame de la Trémouille was no less ardent, and the affair of the pastor Morus led to a disagreement between them. Madame de Turenne and Madame de Bouillon reprobated the celebrated preacher's private life, while Madame de la Trémouille defended him. Turenne, who 'so earnestly desired peace, not only among members of the same church but among the different churches,' was very ill served at home. All this tended insensibly to detach him from Protestantism.

However, he still remained loyal to the practices of the Calvinist form of worship, for he was too religiously minded and too prudent to abandon one confession before he was assured of the excellence of the one that attracted him. But, to avoid all discussion, he and Madame de Turenne went their separate ways in respect to religion. He continued to assist the Protestants

when they were in trouble, and the severity of
the royal orders gave him frequent occasions to
intervene. The best known of his interventions
was in favor of the minister Du Bosc, whose
pardon he obtained after repeating his appeal
to the King for seven months.

We must also refer here to an important document: 'The Vicomte de Turenne's Opinion concerning the So-called Reformed Religion.' This
opinion was requested by the King, who wished
to learn the sentiments of the pastors concerning
the reunion of the two churches. First of all,
Turenne puts the King on his guard against an
excessive zeal which would give an impression of
constraint. He recommends allowing the pastors
to set forth their ideas freely, and avoiding at
any cost the embitterment of the divergences of
opinion by public discussions. He hopes that,
being thus treated with confidence, the Protestants will 'open their minds freely and will come
together in good faith in those matters wherein
they find themselves to be as near the Catholic
religion as the so-called Reformed religion, and
thus it will be an easy step for them to take, to
unite.' The date of this document is not known,
but it is usually placed between 1664 and 1668.
Therein Turenne appears, as always, as a partisan of reunion, tolerant, and realizing things as
they are; a foe of sterile conflicts. It may be that,

when he wrote it, he himself had but one more step to take before joining the Catholic Church. It remains to inquire how he arrived at his decision.

It will be recalled that, when Louis XIV appointed Turenne Maréchal-Général, he gave him to understand that if he chose to be converted, he should be Constable. He had to resist other influences too: it has been said, without proof so far as we are informed, that the Queen-Mother intervened directly and that Mazarin offered him the post of Governor of the Dauphin. But, on the other hand, we know of a certainty that in order to make the siege of Turenne more effective, they attacked his wife and sister, whose influence over him was well known. Barillon, Marquis de Morangis, tried to convert Madame de Turenne to Catholicism, and Anne of Austria tried to bring over the Duchesse de la Trémouille. None of these attempts succeeded, and it is said that Turenne's niece [1] was so distressed at their failure that she took the veil in the hope of obtaining from above the conversion that had been her father's last wish.

Why did Turenne, who had been so long disturbed by religious scruples, who was already in part detached from Protestantism, still hold out,

[1] His brother's daughter who had married a Bavarian prince.

and continue to hold out, for eight more years? We can suggest several reasons for this.

First, his faith was not for sale and the attempts based on offers of material advantage could not fail to retard his decision. A few days after his appointment he wrote to his wife: 'This is what some one asked me yesterday in the greatest secrecy — whether I had offered to change my religion in order to be Constable? You know pretty nearly what I think about all this business.' One likes to place beside this letter the proud response that he made to the King when he requested, a short time after his conversion, his nephew's elevation to the Cardinalate. The King having remarked that the Huguenots would not fail to say that this was his reward, he said, 'I am too well known, Sire, to fear such talk.'

Second, Turenne had a profound affection for those with whom religion placed him in a contradictory position which grew more embittered every day — his wife and his sisters. We have seen how frankly and unreservedly he kept his wife informed as to all that went on in his mind. In the last of his letters to her he expressed his distress at finding himself in disagreement with her as to certain truths which were to him as clear as day; and he added: 'In these matters in which you and my sister and I must act each according to his or her own conscience, we shall be as good friends as ever, thank God! I feel nothing but that in my heart.' Madame de Bouillon died in 1662, then Madame de la Trémouille. Madame de Turenne passed away in 1666. Turenne was deeply afflicted by her death; it severed a strong sentimental bond that bound him to Protestantism. Some thought that he would abjure at once. But Turenne's sturdy intellectual honesty demanded something more than sentiment; it demanded entire faith in the doctrines of the religion toward which he felt drawn. That is the last point that remains to be discussed.

We must not forget that in those days mysticism often kept pace with reason. Pascal was deeply impressed, in 1656, when his little niece was cured by a miracle of the Holy Thorn. Turenne was equally impressed by the one witnessed at the Louvre at the fire that broke out there shortly before Mazarin's death: the flames were arrested by a Blessed Sacrament carried by a priest. 'I saw it,' said Turenne. 'There is no question of my doubting it, I saw it!' This miracle, occurring just when he was striving to find the truth, may have been a very potent helper in the work of persuasion undertaken by those chiefly responsible for his conversion.

175

Many names have been mentioned. Those of Gilbert de Choisel, Bishop of Tournai and friend of M. d'Andilly, and of Vialart de la Herse, Bishop of Châlons, with whom Turenne had frequent interviews. That of Abbé Stuart d'Aubigny, cousin of King Charles II, who had secured the abjuration of the Prince Palatine of Bavaria and who said one day to Turenne: 'If I survive Madame de Turenne, I shall see you in our church'; to which he replied only by a smile. Father Mascaron also had access to the Marshal, and gave him a copy of certain of his sermons so that he might think them over at leisure. Lastly, we must mention, but only to put him aside, the Duc d'Albret, Turenne's nephew and the future Cardinal de Bouillon. He was too young to have the slightest influence over his uncle, who, when he had made up his mind, did not tell him of it until the day of the ceremony. 'You will be very glad,' he said, 'and very angry too; I am going to become a Catholic and I have kept it a secret from you for fear that people would say that you have converted me.'

Port-Royal's attraction for Turenne cannot be denied. His religious training had begun there. 'The Huguenots,' says Choisy, 'favored the Jansenists in everything because of the conformity of their ideas concerning grace.' But the deep-seated cause of the influence of the

Jansenists on his conversion is to be found in the fact that it was in the writings of Nicole and Arnault the Great that he found replies to the publications of the Protestants on the Eucharist, and historical enlightenment on that question. It filled much of his thoughts; he had been greatly struck by the story of a Protestant who had returned to France after having been a slave in Asia Minor, about the belief of the Oriental Christians in the real presence. He had had confirmation of the story from the Chevalier d'Arvieux, who had been in the East; and after his conversion Turenne asked him to collect for him 'all the writings that throw light on this matter.' He had told of the effect produced upon him by reading the 'Traditions of the Church concerning the Eucharist.' The minister Claude replied, at the request, it was said, of Madame de Turenne. Then Nicole, in his turn, published 'The Little Perpetuity' and 'The Great Perpetuity.' This last-named work did not appear until 1669, but Turenne had had it shown him before it was printed. 'What made me leap the ditch and land at the foot of the wall was the first volume in manuscript,' he said to Lionne, who on the day following the conversion repeated the remark to the Cardinal Rospigliosi. D'Ormesson also writes: 'At Monsieur le Prince's they were talking about the reply to the minister Claude's book, and M. de Turenne said that that work had finally persuaded him.' Finally, Saint-Maurice, Ambassador of Savoy, declares that Turenne's conversion was 'a demonstration of the adroitness, learning, and piety of Sieur Arnault.' It is impossible, then, to doubt the determining influence of Port-Royal.

Coming to Bossuet, the exact time at which he began to exert his influence is not known. In 1660 he preached at the Carmelite Convent before the two Queens on the occasion of Turenne's niece's taking the veil. The Marshal was absent, but he was present none the less in the mind of the great bishop. 'Chosen of God to reëstablish the faith in the House of Bouillon,' he said to the novice, speaking of her mother, 'do you follow her exemplary devotion and strive to complete so great a work. You know, my sister, what I have in mind, and however illustrious this assemblage may be, we perceive only too clearly what it lacks. God grant that next year the company may be complete and that that great and unconquerable courage may for once allow itself to be overcome.'

In the ensuing years Turenne had frequent opportunities to meet Bossuet, as they had many mutual friends. Frémont d'Ablancourt speaks of conferences they had, but does not mention the places. Bossuet went frequently to Madame de Longueville's, to see Madame de Conti, her sister-in-law, and it may have been there that those interviews, without witnesses, took place, on matters which were to form the subject of the 'Exposition of the Catholic Faith.' Abbé Ledieu says that this work was written at Turenne's request as he desired to have in writing the lessons he had had by word of mouth. And this statement is confirmed by what Bossuet himself wrote to an English Benedictine, Father Johnston: 'The "Exposition" was written in two sittings; I wrote first the Eucharist and then went on to the rest. I sent the whole to M. de Turenne as I wrote it.' The enlightenment which the Marshal found therein responded to his intellectual cravings; his desire to join the Church was satisfied by Bossuet's arguments reducing to a minimum the differences between Catholics and Protestants; the defense of the Sacraments, and especially of the Eucharist, was a matter that he had much at heart; and finally the affirmation of the authority of the Church was contrasted with an anarchy which he had often deplored. The official edition did not appear until 1671, but Bossuet had had thirteen copies struck off earlier, called 'friends' copies.' When the book appeared in the shops, he requested his friends to send their first copies back to him; all were returned but two: one had fallen into the hands of one of his enemies, the other was Turenne's, who asked his permission to keep it as a remembrance. He loved that book, for the tone was moderate, the exposition simple, the reasoning sincere, and 'it had led him to see the light.'

This time Turenne's hour had come. Something that happened in 1668 was perhaps what brought about the definite decision. That was the conclusion of the Peace of the Church;[1] did it not, by putting an end temporarily to the disputes which had divided the Church in France, sweep away the last scruple which still made Turenne hesitate? 'If he did not declare himself earlier,' writes Saint-Maurice, 'I think that it was from fear of being considered a Jansenist.' It seems nearer the truth to say that he dreaded finding in the Catholic Church the same feuds which had contributed so much to keep it apart from Protestantism.

When Turenne had reached a decision, he went to the Court; it was October 10, 1668, in

---

[1] The phrase 'Peace of the Church' refers to what is usually known as the 'Peace of Clement IX,' when the Jansenists generally were admitted to grace and the interdict was removed from Port-Royal, their headquarters. This peace was only temporary, however, until the death of Madame de Longueville in 1679. The Cistercian Abbey of Port-Royal was founded in the early thirteenth century. Its intimate connection with the Jansenist movement began about 1600.

the afternoon. Frémont d'Ablancourt describes the scene: 'He told the King, who was at table, that he had a word to say to him which he begged His Majesty not to mention. It is, Sire, that I wish to change my religion.' The King thereupon bade the Marshal come to his private apartments and expressed his purpose to send a courier instantly to the Pope, to inform him of the good news, which would give him much pleasure.

'O Sire,' rejoined the Vicomte de Turenne, 'I implore Your Majesty not to do it; for if I believed that this step would put upon my hands the gloves that he wears, I would not take it.'

Turenne made his abjuration on October 23. The very simple ceremony took place in the chapel of the Archbishopric; to avoid the ostentation which would have been inevitable if it had come to the knowledge of the public, he notified only the day before the Archbishop of Paris, in whose hands he placed his profession of faith. Very few persons were present. Of his household, Pertuis, the Captain of the Guards; Desroziers, his maître-d'hôtel; Du Hault, his first valet de chambre; they were Catholics all three, and were deeply moved. Among the others present were Boucherat, Choisy, Abbé Sauvage; the Duc d'Albret was not there. Turenne, after he had abjured, confessed, heard

Mass, and partook of communion at Notre Dame. Thence he went to Saint-Germain, where the King embraced him and the whole Court congratulated him.

Everybody was immensely interested in the event: Catholics to extol him, Protestants to blame him, skeptics to suspect his motives, ambassadors to advise their governments, sometimes with most interesting comments.

Louis XIV, who labored to establish unity of religion in his realm, rejoiced sincerely over so great an example, which he hoped would be followed. The Pope, Clement IX, had been informed by a special courier from the Duc d'Albret; no news could more fittingly put the finishing touch to the Peace of the Church so far as Rome was concerned.

It was natural that the Protestants should regret this desertion of their faith as an act of treachery. The most exasperated of them spared Turenne neither libelous attacks nor ballads; they accused him of being led astray by his ambition to be named King of Poland, or by his disappointment at having failed to carry out his scheme of creating, with the aid of the Huguenots, a republic of which he should be the head. All this was not very reasonable and is hardly worth mention. But we must add that even the most cultured and the most moderate of his former coreligionists had little belief in the sincerity of his sentiments. Moreover, all those who were offended by Turenne's influence feared lest he become more powerful after his conversion, and accused him of having been converted for selfish motives. This charge deserves to be examined.

When he was still young, having his whole future to provide for, which an alliance with Richelieu or Mazarin would have facilitated enormously, and being well aware, too, how serious an obstacle to his promotion his religion was in the King's eyes, he had resisted all approaches. And would he have given way at fifty-seven, when he had no higher position to work for, no honor to covet, and when he had just conducted a victorious campaign during which he acted as the King's prompter and adviser, so closely heeded that courtiers and ministers were frantic with jealousy? That would be hard to understand, indeed.

But, some one may say, he still had to make provision for his nephews and nieces. It is true that in the years immediately following his conversion one of his nieces married a prince of Bavaria and the Duc d'Albret was made a Cardinal. As to the marriage, we need say simply that, at the time of the Portuguese plan, the King had shown an equal desire to gratify Turenne.

As for the cardinal's hat bestowed on him who was to be known as the 'Red Child,' because he was but twenty-six when it was placed on his head, that was a most complicated and, we may add, a most trivial business. It originated in the rivalry between the Bouillons and the Le Telliers. Louvois's elder brother and the Duc d'Albret, churchmen both, were of about the same age and equally ambitious. Their rivalry, begun at the Sorbonne, became more intense in the race for appointments and privileges, and, Charles Maurice Le Tellier having been appointed coadjutor to the Archbishop of Rheims, the Duc d'Albret induced his uncle to request for him the coadjutorship to the Archbishop of Paris. Turenne obtained the Archbishop's assent, but was refused that of the King, 'who,' says Choisy, 'had not forgotten the war in Paris in which the then Coadjutor, Cardinal de Retz, had given him so much trouble.' But Louis XIV having assured Turenne that he would comply with any other request of his, he asked for the cardinal's hat for his nephew, which the King promised, thinking that it would be a long time before the appointment would have to be made.

Circumstances favored the Duc d'Albret; the Peace of the Church, and assistance extended by France to Crete, made the Holy See favorably inclined. Urgent representations were made at

Rome by the King himself, who was anxious to divert attention from the too rapid promotion of Abbé Le Tellier. Lionne, too, put in a word with Cardinal Rospigliosi and the Pope. Matters appeared to be thoroughly prepared, Choisy tells us, when Cardinal Rospigliosi wrote to Lionne that if the King chose to give the appointment to M. de Turenne himself, the Pope would ratify it as soon as the courier arrived. M. de Lionne read Cardinal Rospigliosi's letter to M. de Turenne and cited the recent example of the Cardinal of Vendôme. 'Oh, Monsieur,' rejoined Turenne, 'what should I do with a cardinal's hat and a long cue? That costume would be a great burden to me. I beg you to thank the Pope for me and to request him to make my nephew a cardinal.' M. de Lionne reported this to the King, who said: 'I should have been much surprised if M. de Turenne had bitten at that suggestion.' Turenne did not allow himself to be turned aside for a moment; he said to the Duc d'Albret: 'You have a very dangerous competitor for the cardinalate. The King has only to nominate him and the Pope offers to make him cardinal on the arrival of the courier. But don't be alarmed,' he added, 'that competitor is myself.'

At the same time Turenne had sent a reply to the Pope, thanking him and apologizing for his refusal, 'because his whole life had been devoted to concerns of a different nature and he was resolved to make no change in his mode of living.' The Duc d'Albret was made a cardinal in August, 1669.

As a matter of fact, we may go even further and agree with Choisy that, if Turenne became a convert from selfish motives, he reckoned badly, for as a Catholic he was simply lost in the multitude of courtiers, whereas, as a Protestant, a moral leader, and often the spokesman of his coreligionists, he would have continued to be a personage to be reckoned with.

Seven years after Turenne's death, Arnault the Great answered thus the questions of the Protestants: 'What did M. de Turenne gain by turning Catholic? Did he not command the King's army when he was still a Huguenot? What has he had since that he had not then? Has he become richer? On the contrary, every one knows that he died poor.' This reply seems to close the discussion.

Turenne's convictions became manifestly stronger in the light of the way in which he practiced the Catholic religion after his conversion. Madame de Sévigné tells us that, Turenne having asked his nephew if he could not receive communion at Pentecost without confessing, he told him no and that 'he could hardly be sure that he had not offended God since Easter. He told him his story; he was not within a thousand leagues of a mortal sin. However, he went to confession because it was the custom. He said: "But must I tell that Recollet everything just as I would M. de Saint-Gervais?" In truth, such a soul is well deserving of Heaven.'

This tale, which perhaps the Cardinal de Bouillon embroidered a little to make it more edifying, reveals at the same time Turenne's ingenuousness and his wish to avoid confession — a survival of his former religion. In his last campaigns he was accompanied by a priest of the Oratory, in the capacity of almoner, and Madame de Sévigné, who had it from one of her attendants, tells us that on the day he was killed, 'he intended to confess and that he was to attend communion the next day.'

We know, furthermore, from several sources that in 1674 Turenne planned to return to the Oratory, to end his days there. He had spoken of this purpose to Desroziers, his maître-d'hôtel, who was himself to die at the Oratory. One of the officers for whom he had the greatest affection, M. de Chédigny, had already betaken himself thither several years earlier and was in correspondence with him. It is not improbable that Turenne, serious-minded and meditative as he was, who did nothing by halves and who in the last years had discovered all that there is of vanity and illusion in human satisfaction, had turned to the thought of making ready for death by a definitive retirement. Louis XIV would not allow it, and it was at the King's instance that he postponed the execution of his plans until after the campaign of 1675.

After he became a Catholic, Turenne persisted in his desire for the union of the two churches, and he exerted himself in every possible way to achieve so difficult an end. He gave his support to the collection of funds to assist converted ministers. In his will there were legacies of thirty thousand livres for the poor of each of the towns of Sedan, Nègrepelisse, and Castellan, who should be converted. This religious fervor went side by side with the broadest toleration; he continued to believe that people must be led by persuasion, not by violence, and he had the courage to say to the King: 'Sire, since I have belonged to the community of the R. P. R.[1] I have never before been able to give Your Majesty my opinion; but now I can say that, if you should consent to their massacre, you would do the Pope a great service, but you would do yourself a great disservice.'

We can then approach and carry on to the end our study of Turenne's conversion without the

[1] Reformed Protestant Religion.

188

fear of finding therein any act or thought which degraded him. He had a most intense inward life, and for that reason he was led in his early years to reflect upon religious problems, even to the point of taking with him on his campaigns books treating those problems. From the moment when he began to have doubts of the religion in which he had been brought up, he started to ascertain where the truth lay, and neglected nothing that would help him to find it. When he believed that he had found it, he went to it simply, drawn by it alone. He devoted himself with ardor to the religion he had embraced. He continued to defend his former coreligionists, and his toleration brought forth this well-deserved judgment of Saint-Évremond: 'As a Huguenot, he had in his heart nothing contrary to the interests of Catholics; when converted, he displayed no zeal prejudicial to the safety of Huguenots.'

'M. de Turenne's conversion was the more honorable to himself and to the Church in that it cannot be suspected of any human interest; the truth of our religion has all the glory of it.' So says Bussy, who was long an enemy of Turenne's. So must we all think after following him through all the phases of this great moral crisis.

Chapter V

WAR WITH HOLLAND: TURENNE UNDER
LOUIS XIV AND UNDER LOUVOIS

In January, 1672, Louis XIV informed Vauban that he had an escort that would enable him to 'travel in Holland without apprehension.' It was, in fact, at the head of 120,000 men that he was about to take the field.

With the methods in vogue at that time, it was not possible to maneuver so large a force in a single body, but it was necessary to distribute it into several corps, each under its own leader; and, as each of the operations of these corps looked to the same end, these leaders must be subject to a common authority. So long as the King was with the army, it was he who exercised the supreme command, and no question arose; but when government affairs called him away, it was of the utmost necessity that the devolution of the command should be settled beforehand, and we have seen that the order of succession as between officers of the same rank had not been adjusted.

For this reason Louis XIV decided that for the campaign of 1672 the ranking order should be as follows: immediately after the King, Monsieur, then the Prince de Condé, then the Vicomte de

Turenne, and after him the other marshals in order of seniority. So far as the royal family and the first Prince of the Blood (Condé) were concerned, this seemed natural enough. But the Maréchals de Bellefonds, d'Humières, and de Créqui, to whom the King's decision applied, would not consent to be placed under Turenne. They would have consented to obey a Constable, but they did not recognize the authority of a Maréchal-Général; Turenne's 'princery' did not seem to them a sufficient title; nor did the age and gallantry of the great captain, who, moreover, as Bussy admits, 'was commanding armies when these gentry were in school, and who taught them what little they know.' The other marshals thereupon refused to obey the King's order.

Louis XIV appealed first to Bellefonds, to whom he was much attached. Bellefonds persisted in his refusal, claiming that 'he should be dishonored by this unprecedented submission,' and that 'he could not obey the orders of M. de Turenne without derogating from the rank to which the King had raised him.' The King exiled him to Tours and struck his name from the list of his household. D'Humières declared that he would follow the example of his fellows, and he had to retire to Mouchy. While awaiting the arrival of Créqui, for whom he had sent, Louis XIV asked the opinion of Maréchal du Plessis-Praslin, who replied that it was without precedent that a marshal of France should be commanded by one of his fellows; that all regarded Turenne as 'the most illustrious man alive; but that, if His Majesty insisted that all should obey him, he must make M. de Turenne Constable.' When Créqui arrived, he was even more intractable, offering to surrender his marshal's bâton and serve as a volunteer. The King sent him away 'to plant cabbages at one of his houses.'

Louis XIV shrewdly took note of the shades of difference in their opposition, saying that Belle-fonds had refused brutally, D'Humières idiot-ically, and Créqui with spirit; but he treated them with equal severity. He was inexorable until they had made due submission. When they declared themselves ready to submit, he ordered them to serve fifteen days each as lieutenant-general under Turenne.

Although this whole business directly con-cerned him, Turenne had kept entirely out of it. In the last months of 1672 he received the King's instructions to see to it that Maréchals de Créqui and d'Humières were recognized as lieutenant-generals, to have them serve as officer of the day alternately, and to make use of them to the best advantage for the King's service. Turenne treated them with his customary sim-plicity and kindness, received them courteously, and even offered them a guard, which they refused; and he was able to report to the King that 'it had passed off very civilly.'

Thus ended the 'quarrel of the marshals.' It made much noise and gave rise to most contradictory judgments, some blaming the marshals, others pitying them for not having been able to act differently without dishonoring themselves. Madame de Sévigné wrote: 'This is the only thing that people are talking about; some say that they have done right, others that they have done wrong; the Comtesse de Fiesque shouts herself hoarse, the Comte de Guichet resorts to his falsetto; they have to be separated; it is a regular farce.' The diversity of these opinions shows how essential it was to establish rules of the hierarchical order, and how well-advised the King was to be so firm. It was necessary for him to enforce discipline upon those nobles who regarded discipline as unnecessary, since, without it, they met death so valiantly in his service. And it was Louis XIV unaided who held his ground so stoutly, for in this contest Louvois behaved very cannily.

The Minister had no interest in doing a disservice to persons who were already in the sovereign's ill graces. He reserved his shafts for those who were in favor at Court and who might bear him a grudge. In these last years, as his authority increased, he appeared to be 'at the highest point of influence and arrogance, and claimed the right to be addressed as "Monseigneur."' He assumed to deny that title to Turenne, to whom it was accorded by all, while many called him 'Highness.' The Marshal appealed to the King, who ordered that the House of Bouillon should retain the 'Monseigneur' of the Secretaries of State. We mention this trifling matter, which was of more importance at the time than one would imagine, because it shows what the relations between Turenne and Louvois were at the beginning of the war with Holland.

Never had so powerful a French army been opposed to so weak an adversary. So the campaign of 1672 was justly called a military promenade, and it presents no interest from the standpoint of military operations. But it does mark the beginning of a new régime, and by following its development we shall see how Turenne adapted himself to the King's personal management of affairs, which was manifested sometimes directly and sometimes through the medium of his Minister.

The forces assembled in May on the Sambre were divided into three armies: one, under Luxembourg, was to operate in Westphalia; Condé commanded the second, and Turenne the third, under the immediate orders of the King and

Monsieur; both were to operate in the Low Countries. Condé wanted to lay siege to Maestricht, the possession of which he considered indispensable; Turenne, thinking that the siege would be a long one and would give the Dutch time to receive support from their allies, advised isolating the place and taking the bulk of the forces toward the Lower Rhine, in order to open the road into Holland speedily. His advice prevailed and the towns along the Rhine fell in quick succession.

As they were about to enter Holland there was another conference: Condé was in favor of forcing by direct attack the lines of the Yssel, which were defended by the greater part of the forces of the Prince of Orange, while Turenne was in favor of continuing along the Rhine, to attack the enemy's rear. This last plan was adopted; it led to the famous crossing of the Rhine, a really trivial affair which caused a tremendous sensation and was glorified as one of the greatest events of the reign. Condé was wounded in the skirmish brought about by the rashness of the young Ducs d'Enghien and de Longueville, which cost the latter his life.

After Condé was wounded, the King sent for the Duc d'Enghien, and gave Turenne command of the army that was operating by itself. But while he was delayed by the necessity of occupying all the forts on the Yssel, which fell without resistance, the Dutch cut the dykes and let in the waters to save their country. Then, after the people, driven frantic by their suffering, had massacred Cornelius and Jan de Witt, the Stadholdership was revived in favor of the Prince of Orange. The resistance of Holland thereupon entered a new phase. She also was to benefit by the errors of Louis XIV.

The King, wasting precious time, had not occupied the center of the dyke system at Minden, and had not marched upon Amsterdam. He had made himself as powerless as his adversary by scattering his infantry among the fortresses, despite the advice of Turenne and Condé to keep only the chief ones, and to pull down the others and save the bulk of the troops for operations. 'The King,' said Louvois to the contrary, 'had troops enough to retain the forts and hold the enemy in check.' And this time Louis XIV believed the man who flattered him. He had agreed to exchange thirty thousand Dutch prisoners for a ransom of two hundred crowns per man, which transaction gave the Prince of Orange an army for a song. Lastly, and most important, he had, in accord with Louvois, disdainfully refused the proposals brought to his camp by the Dutch envoys — proposals which, it seems, Turenne was in favor of accepting. For the sake of illusory

196

advantages, Louis XIV alarmed all Europe by
his power and his spirit of conquest.

The King left the army on July 12, leaving
Turenne in command, with instructions which
ordered him to watch the movements of the
Emperor and the princes of the Empire. At the
end of August the troops of the Elector of Brandenburg having joined those of the Emperor,
the King ordered Turenne to cross the Rhine.
The German princes who were allies of France
demanded at once that the Marshal should attack. But he, determined 'to govern his movements by looking far ahead,' and not to destroy
his troops to no purpose, did not move. The
idlers at Court blamed his inaction. Louvois re-
proved him and told him of the King's anxieties
and of the chagrin he felt at finding that his
orders were not executed.

In October, the King having demanded a
victory in the shortest possible time, Louvois annotated this order in words which are worth
quoting: 'I think it needless to tell you how
much His Majesty would be injured by the ill
success of his army; so I will say nothing on that
subject, and will add simply, that, by this remark which His Majesty has ordered me to make
to you, he does not intend to compel you to
guarantee results, but simply to place you in a

position to make up your mind, and to give you to understand that you are not to attack these troops except in case the full knowledge that you possess of their numbers and their quality shall give you reasons to believe that you can safely offer battle when you shall have resolved to fight.' Possessed of such pathetically vague incoherent instructions, Turenne had only to follow his own inclination, and that is what he did.

But Louvois harassed him, and in fact restrained his freedom of action by criticizing a halt here, suggesting a march there, and haggling over trifles. Instead of sending him the reenforcements that were indispensable for an offensive movement, he urged him to reduce his own force for the benefit of Condé, while continuing to protest against his silence and immobility, and even making insinuations about his timidity in an almost daily correspondence and with great bitterness of tone.

Turenne, who had at first kept calm under it all, lost his patience at last. Replying on November 9 to a letter from Louvois, he gave him in detail the reasons that prevented his carrying out a maneuver suggested from Paris, and could not resist adding: 'If you were here on the spot, you would laugh at such an idea.' As Louvois insisted, he explained himself freely and with dignity concerning his silence. 'It is true that I have been guilty of this fault — when I think that a thing cannot or should not be done, and am persuaded that the King, who is my commander, would change his opinion if he saw the condition of things, I do not give my reasons.'

But these annoyances did not prevent his keeping his eye on the enemy, and when, late in November, the Dutch Imperial troops tried to join forces, he moved at one bound upon the Moselle, thus placing himself between the allies. This maneuver was not understood at Paris, where naturally something better was hoped for; 'so that,' he writes, 'if one were not content with the assurance that one loves better to serve the King than anything else in the world, one would lose one's head between the easy jobs that they envisage from a long way off and the difficulties that loom up on the spot.'

But his head was not one of those that get lost, and a few days later he repeated in another form: 'One can do only those things that are practicable when the time comes; that is all that the King can ask of those who serve him.' In the end he took a higher tone, and on December 17 he dealt Louvois a decided counterblast: 'You are well aware, Monsieur, that experience leads us to say as to certain things that they cannot be done; although I have no very high opinion of myself, I should deem myself unfit to serve the King if he could not place a little reliance upon what I say.'

At all events, and that fact alone was much in his favor, Turenne had succeeded in preventing the junction of the two hostile forces. Louis XIV acknowledged later that 'this maneuver succeeded perfectly well'; but at the same moment he gave way to a momentary outburst of ill-humor: 'I could have wished that you had carried out the order I gave you, but — I let my mind rest upon my confidence in you.' Turenne asked nothing more.

Thus ended the year 1672.

At the beginning of the following year, the King, intent upon his summer campaign, wished to keep Turenne's troops at rest. But the Marshal believed that there were great results to be obtained, and he cleverly brought the King and Louvois around to his way of thinking. Here are some extracts from his letters:

'January 4. As M. de Munster strongly urges me, I propose to go personally to Wesel — and I shall judge from what I learn of the enemy and of the condition of M. de Munster's troops what I think it best to do.'

On the 7th, he has seen and decided: 'I think it very important for the King's service that I cross the Rhine in sufficient force to prevent the

Germans from spreading to Westphalia and even to drive them back across the Weser River, if possible.'

On the 9th, he goes further into this plan: 'I think that nothing is of more capital importance for the King's service than to try not to give the Germans any rest between here and the Weser; this will involve consequences for the impending campaign which the King sees better than I, and which you, Monsieur, saw very clearly.'

On the 12th, he waves aside objections and widens his horizon: 'In Germany they make the same progress in winter as in summer, when they have no army opposing them. I shall act on the lines I have laid down, being persuaded that it is the King's desire to try so to conduct affairs that his arms shall retain their reputation, which, in my opinion, will not happen without some decisive action.'

On the 16th, he utters this momentous sentence: 'This can be done only by putting ourselves in condition to give battle'; and in order to appease beforehand the impatience that he knows so well, he concludes: 'In the delay in construction of the bridge because of the wind, in the difficulty about forage and quarters for the troops, it is impossible to say definitely what we shall do, having before us a hostile country and an enemy.'

On the 19th, his pleasant anticipations were

confirmed: 'I don't mean to flatter myself, but I think that things are going very well, indeed.'

Finally, on the 29th, he feels that he has won his game, and he drives home his advantage, calling for reënforcements, 'for the King will see that we cannot make war by halves.'

And as, meanwhile, Turenne had been successful in his first movement, Louvois humbled himself so far as to write to him: 'Having explained to you all His Majesty's thoughts, he leaves it to you to do whatever you consider most advantageous for his service.' His earlier experiences had not been without result.

Turenne showed himself worthy of the King's trust. He marched straightway upon the Great Elector and forced him to break his camp, leaving behind a part of his heavy artillery, and pursued him notwithstanding the ice and snow. He crossed the Weser, and by that audacious maneuver compelled the Imperial army to withdraw into Franconia, and the Great Elector to retire to Berlin and sign terms of peace.

These auspicious events aroused lively enthusiasm at Court. The King was not sparing of compliments to their author. To those which Louvois, too, thought fit to pay him, he replied simply: 'You write me that the King is content with what has been done here, of which I am very glad because it was my sole aim. You also, in your individual capacity, pay me a compliment for which I offer you my most humble thanks.'

These successes were to enable Louis XIV, by the capture of Maestricht, to strike a blow from which he anticipated important political results. Meanwhile, Turenne, on the Rhine, was to hold the Imperial forces in check. This was destined to be a very distressing campaign for the Marshal, both because of obstacles of all sorts and because of the helpless state to which he was finally reduced.

At the outset, he found his forces reduced by a fourth for the behoof of the King's army. On the morrow of the capture of Maestricht, he asked for reënforcements; but the King, whose mind was on Franche-Comté, refused him, thus making it impossible for him to undertake anything. Meanwhile, Louvois had gone back to his old methods, and the Marshal wrote to him: 'I see clearly the King's purposes and will do my best to conform to them; but you will allow me to say to you that I do not think it for His Majesty's interests to give such definite orders from so great a distance to the most incapable man in France.' These words have caused him to be accused of infraction of discipline and of injustice to Louvois. We shall recur to this subject.

Their relations were not improved by the proceedings of the intendants. Turenne dismissed Charuel, Louvois's confidential agent, 'whose writings are very dangerous,' but his successor continued to give Louvois information in secret.

On the other hand, Louvois and the King himself blamed Turenne for the depredations of which the troops were guilty. Turenne has sometimes been criticized very severely for these doings, and his kindness to his soldiers contrasted with his indifference to the sufferings of the conquered peoples. So that the subject is worth a moment's consideration. We have had occasion to observe that the devastation of a country was one of the means resorted to for the reduction of an enemy, and it will be remembered that Mazarin congratulated Turenne on having fed his army so well without asking for a sou. Governments then were very indulgent in regard to such excesses and paid no heed to them unless compelled by diplomatic emergencies.

Moreover, during this same war, it was the King and his Minister who ordered this sort of thing to be done. 'I desire,' Louis XIV wrote to Turenne in 1672, 'that you should send troops into the County of La Marck as into a hostile country, and by the money you will get from them and by the disorder you will stir up there, you should put the County in such a condition

that the troops can find no subsistence there.'
— 'You will spare in so far as you can, the estates
of the princes who are in alliance with His Majesty,' wrote Louvois in 1673, 'and with regard
to the near-by estates belonging to princes acting
in the Emperor's interest, you will have much
less consideration for them; and you will have
very little for the estates belonging to M. de
Trèves.'

It can be imagined that it is very difficult to
release and restrain at will the passions of soldiers
often underpaid and ill fed; and Turenne rea-
soned justly in his reply to an envoy from the
King to a German prince: 'I will do, so far as I
am concerned, all that I can to reconcile two
things so different as to remain in Germany until we have assurance from the Empire and to
manage so that the Empire will be content with
our choice of persons whose estates we subsist
on.'

Such practices, detestable as they are, were
upheld by the political morality of the time, and
sixteen years later Louvois ordered the sys-
tematic pillaging of the Palatinate. Since then
most belligerents have abandoned them; in our
day only one nation has incorporated them in
its military teaching and utilized the progress
of science to apply them more rigorously and
cruelly than ever.

The capture of Maestricht had revived the fighting spirit of the allies. Montecuculli crossed the Rhine unexpectedly and by so doing forced Turenne to recross the river. Louvois did not miss the point; 'The King has learned that his affairs in Germany are not in so advantageous a state as might be desired; it is disappointing to advance only to be insulted by having to fall back so far.' Turenne saw clearly that a defeat was to be expected, and did not fail to warn Louvois that Bonn was threatened and that he himself was in no condition to defend it. The place, being weakly defended, fell on November 12.

Louvois would have had Turenne attempt to recapture it, but everything combined to make it impossible — the small number and the condition of his troops, the lack of supplies, the state of the roads, and the season. The Marshal decided that he could go no farther than the Moselle, and he held to that decision, opposing the King's wishes, letters of Louvois, the criticisms of the Court, of which he heard the echo, and the outcries of the French diplomats stationed in Germany. He was even compelled — and this must have been especially painful to him — to contend with malcontents in his own army; one of his lieutenant-generals, Saint-Abre — a very gallant officer, by the way — said aloud that they ought to go after the enemy. Turenne having retorted, 'Write to the Court, Monsieur; your reasons, however bad, will surely be listened to there,' the King was deeply moved and did justice to the conduct of the Marshal, who was generous enough to speak highly of Saint-Abre and to take him back into his army the next year.

Turenne had returned to Paris in December, exasperated by all the petty annoyances he had had to endure, but especially because he had seen the campaign, which had begun so well, brought to an end by a check which it would have been easy to avoid by a wiser employment of the troops set free by the capture of Maestricht. Condé, like him, was disgusted by the conduct of the Ministers and dissatisfied, too, with the obscure part they had allotted to him; and they agreed to carry their complaints to the King together, but in the end Condé consented to let Turenne present his demand alone. The interview took place early in 1674. Turenne, according to Villars, 'laid before the King the blunders of M. de Louvois, the lack of definiteness in the orders he had received from him. M. de Louvois had much intelligence, was excellent in matters of detail, but lacked entirely the knowledge and experience necessary for the conduct of a campaign.' Moreover, he accused Louvois of having concealed from the King certain of his letters, and asked that he might receive no orders in the future except from the King and might correspond only with him.

The Court and the city were much excited over this controversy, which the ballad-writers treated after their fashion:

> Le Vicomte dit à Louvois
> Ce que toute la terre en pense,
> Car il osa dire au Roi
> Que tous les maux de la France
> Ce petit-fils de Procureur
> En était la cause et l'auteur.
> Au Connêtable insolent
> Qui fait le petit Dieu sur terre
> Il lui dit effectivement
> Qu'il n'était point homme de guerre
> Et qu'il ferait mieux le metier
> De commissaire de quartier.[1]

Louvois was fain to pay Turenne a visit of apology, which gave no satisfaction to either. Turenne succeeded further in obtaining an order that all his correspondence to the King should pass through the hands of the Cardinal de Bouillon. Saint-Simon, who gives us this information, adds that the advantage of this order was

[1] The Vicomte told Louvois what the whole world thinks of him, for he dared to say to the King that this grandson of an attorney was the cause and instigator of all the ills of France. To the overbearing Constable, who enacts the little God on earth, he said flatly that he was no fighting man and that he would do better at the trade of errand boy.

imaginary, because Louvois saw Turenne's letters and advised the King about his replies. In fact, Louis XIV could no more do without Louvois's services than without Turenne's, and he knew what to expect from the lack of discretion and the pretensions of the one and the touchy spirit of independence of the other.

Was Turenne, then, one of those great nobles who would not agree to be bound by any rules, or did his military triumphs so puff up his pride that he considered all discipline beneath him? By no means; to judge his conduct fairly, we must consider what the relations between the government and the High Command should be.

Louis XIV and Louvois were justified in their claim that it was for them to decide upon the objects of the military policy and that the military leaders were simply executants. They were right in trying to impose mental discipline upon them as well as in requiring that they make reports of their acts. But they erred in not confining themselves to commands of a general nature and in giving to the leader of an army — *a fortiori* to a Turenne — detailed orders for operations to be carried out two hundred leagues from Versailles. By so doing they invited disobedience when they had to do with a man of high courage and resolution, or disaster when

209

they were dealing with a courtier. Each man to his job: to the government the privilege of setting forth by general orders the results to be obtained; to the military leader the duty of conforming to the general orders, and the formidable honor of acting on his own responsibility, but with complete liberty of action to lead his troops to victory.

The royal power, which had just been reëstablished, had had neither time nor opportunity to set bounds to its own authority, which would permit the initiative of subordinates to develop within clearly defined limits. Fearful of not being obeyed, it was wielded as a single unit without distinction. But it is necessary to distinguish between the King, who was possessed of a natural authority and was already sufficiently sure of himself to command in the broad sense, and his overbearing Minister, an extreme partisan of the centralization of power, who desired to lay down rules for the conduct of the campaign as if it were a matter of allotting lodgings or filling a magazine storehouse. This is so true that on every page of the correspondence of Louvois we find this contradiction between the breadth of view of Louis XIV and the Minister's cocksureness, which restricts in the same sentence the freedom of action he has just conceded in his master's name.

Hence, that manner of exercising the command

against which Turenne protested, and he did it,
let us observe, by appealing always to the King
from his Minister even when he was addressing
the latter. He did not refuse to obey, but he
proposed to conform, not to the letter, but to the
spirit of the instructions he received, and to reserve his liberty to choose the most favorable
moment for their execution. As for the orders as
to matters of detail, issued at a distance, which
could hardly apply either to the places or the
circumstances involved, Turenne did not carry
them out because they were impossible to carry
out. Most of the time Louvois did not understand, and lost his temper; he did not know how
to command commanders and he treated as on
the same level — a very common mistake — the
obedience of a servant and that of a marshal of
France. Feeling that he was misunderstood, and
being averse to the idea of justifying himself as
to things that had gone before, fearing indis-
cretion on the part of the Court if he should reveal his future plans, Turenne took refuge in
silence and waited until events should prove him
to be in the right.

Thus the conflict between Turenne and Louvois was something more than a question of personal rivalry: its subject was of much higher import, for the very doctrine of the High Command
was at stake. Let us remember, too, that be-

211

tween Turenne whose policy it was to fight, and the majority of his contemporaries who preferred sieges, the whole doctrine of war also was in issue, and that fact was not of a nature to lessen their misunderstanding.

CHAPTER VI

THE LAST AND THE BEST OF TURENNE'S
CAMPAIGNS

THE campaign of 1674 opened under unfavorable auspices, the hostile coalition having rounded itself out by the adhesion of England and the greater part of Germany.

The King had decided to strike at the outset, and in person, the principal blow in Franche-Comté. Condé was to shield him on the north against the Prince of Orange, and Turenne, on the Rhine, against the Germans. The plan seemed to assign only an unimportant rôle to Turenne. Such was the opinion of Louvois, who wrote that 'M. de Turenne is apprehensive of being of no use in the campaign,' and of Villars, who observed that Turenne was 'placed in charge of affairs on the Rhine, but with such scanty forces that it seemed as if they relied upon his ability alone.' Turenne had the same idea, and said to Primi Visconti that 'the Court left him with few troops, as his enemies believed that he would under those conditions be placed in a perilous situation.' Let us say simply this: that Louvois had no reason to desire that Turenne should acquire any greater glory, and that the

213

King, desirous to assure himself an easy and speedy triumph, did not understand, as Turenne himself did, the importance of protecting Alsace and Lorraine. Events were soon to prove it, and to give the Marshal a part to play in the foreground.

In a few weeks the King occupied the whole of Franche-Comté, while, by a swift maneuver in Upper Alsace, although deprived of part of his troops, so that Condé could engineer 'some fine siege,' Turenne prevented the Duke of Lorraine from crossing the Rhine.

But the Marshal anticipated more serious danger, and as soon as the King's success was assured, he called his attention to the importance of the theater of operations of which he was in charge. In a letter of June 4, he enumerated the hostile forces that he might soon have in front of him, emphasized the risk to be run if he were left to face them without support, and added: 'In Flanders one lays his course according to his strength; but in this country one must either fight or lose a province. I refer mainly to Alsace, which is of such vital importance that if the enemy were in possession of it, he would have Philipsburg and Brisach behind him and Lorraine and the Messin country would be open to him. This is to repeat — since Your Majesty is pleased that I should say what I think — that you should station a body of troops at Châlons, from which place it could throw its weight into the scale in whichever direction you should see that it was most important. I do not believe that M. le Prince approves of undertaking an extensive siege, for even if it should be successful we should be risking everything else for a single fortress, and in view of the present condition of affairs in Germany, and of the composition of the Empire, I think that I am in duty bound to lay before Your Majesty the consequences. Even if I had the honor to command in this section I should speak just as I do.'

In this letter Turenne writes like a great military commander. In these few lines he estimates the relative importance of the various theaters of operation, points out the course to be followed in each of them, and suggests to the King the best use to make of his reserves; once more he advises against a war of sieges and he enounces his ruling idea, the idea of defending by taking the offensive, which he was constantly to uphold and put in practice throughout that admirable campaign. Then, with that comprehension of realities which characterizes him, he writes the same day to Louvois, to ask that the forts of Haguenau and Saverne, which he expects to make the pivots of his maneuvers, might be garrisoned. Relieved from this anxious preoccupation, he returns on

June 11, in a letter to the Minister, to the main theme of his letter to the King: 'If the King had taken the greatest fortress in Flanders and the Emperor was in possession of Alsace, in my opinion the King's affairs would be in the worst possible condition; for the Germans would have Strassburg with them and all Germany behind them, and you can see what armies they would have in Lorraine, the Bishoprics, and Champagne.'

Turenne secured the dispatch to Trèves of a corps of observation, which, under Rochefort, was to defend the valley of the Moselle, and, if need should arise, join him.

While looking ahead and striving to induce the King to consent to sending the reënforcements necessary for the future, the Marshal did not lose sight of the present. Learning that the Duke of Lorraine was coming down the right bank of the Rhine, to join Bournonville, who was on his way from Frankfurt with the Imperial troops, he determined, on that same 11th of June, to cross the Rhine and prevent their junction. On the 12th, he left Haguenau with a small force, unencumbered, and on his way, at Philipsburg, took six guns and more troops. On the 16th, at Sinzheim, he overtook the Lorrainers, who, holding a strong position on the plateau overlooking the stream,

216

resisted the crossing of the Elsatz. Turenne crossed by sheer force and occupied points of support that the enemy had overlooked. Supported on this base, he deployed his army and out-maneuvered the enemy, who finally disbanded in the woods, leaving two thousand men on the field. 'I have fought no battles in Germany,' he writes, 'where the enemy was more thoroughly dispersed.'

In five days he had marched thirty-five leagues, crossed the Rhine, overtaken, surprised, and beaten a foe who had a great advantage over him. A medal, bearing streaks of lightning, surrounded by the inscription *Vis et celeritas*, was struck in commemoration of this victory of Sinzheim, which was due entirely to his genius for quick decision and to the rapidity of his movements.

This success gave him a little respite, although the Lorrainers and Imperialists succeeded in joining forces. He moved here and there along the Rhine, to keep them in suspense, on the alert to take advantage of a blunder by attacking them. But he neither could nor would make any promises to the Court. 'One finds things so different from what one thought that there is no pleasure in arousing false hopes.'

Meanwhile, the main effort of the coalition was

directed against the Prince de Condé in Flanders. The King wished that Turenne, leaving only a few troops in Alsace, should march to the Moselle, in order to be at hand to support Condé. Turenne objected, for he was already facing superior forces which might be reënforced any day by those of the Elector of Brandenburg. On August 4, the King, being very anxious, wrote to Turenne to ask his opinion, not concerning an immediate evacuation of Alsace, but concerning the eventual dismantling of the fortresses of Alsace except Brisach and Philipsburg, and retiring into Lorraine. Turenne replied on the 8th, begging him first of all to believe that 'if the enemy held Alsace, having Strassburg behind him, he would carry the war into Lorraine and Champagne, and in a few days they would have to be thinking about supporting Toul.' Then, passing rapidly over the technical questions, 'for it would require a book rather than a letter to state all the arguments,' he asked His Majesty 'to send to Saverne the troops remaining in Lorraine,' and to let him 'manage as well as he could.' Finally, assuming a still higher tone, he concluded: 'I will say to Your Majesty that it would be better for your service that I should lose a battle than that I should recross the mountains and abandon Alsace. You know how many troops you have. I beg you, in these three months which will bring your affairs into good or evil case, not to send them except to those places where they will be able to serve some purpose of the first importance. *Provided that one has a reasonable number of troops, one does not leave a country, although the enemy is the stronger.*'

The great general gave that day to the master who had been his pupil a useful lesson, which was not wasted. Thirty-five years later Louis XIV wrote to Maréchal de Villars, at a moment of very great anxiety, the admirable letter in which he said, 'I know all the arguments of the courtiers; almost all of them want me to withdraw to Blois and not to wait until the enemy's army approaches Paris. For my part *I know that armies so large as mine are never so thoroughly defeated that the greater part of them cannot fall back on the Somme.*'

Turenne's advice prevailed. However, the victory that Condé won at Seneffe in Flanders, on August 10, saved northern France from invasion and allowed the King to reënforce Turenne. The Rhine became once more the chief field of interest.

But the coalition forces also were reënforced and faced Turenne's twenty thousand men with thirty-seven thousand. Luckily there was not a good understanding among them and, so Turenne writes to Abbé de Gravel, 'no man can be more disgusted with another than the Duc de Lorraine is with the Duc de Bournonville.' Their maneuvers reflected the condition of affairs, and Turenne foiled them without overmuch difficulty.

The coalition forces then decided to march upon Strassburg by the bridge at Kehl. As soon as he had detected their plan, Turenne set arms and diplomacy at work together: through his Intendant Machault he secured a promise of neutrality from the magistrates of Strassburg, and he sent Vauban with a strong advance-guard to hold the bridge of Kehl. But, in order to avoid bringing on a rupture with the Strassburgers, Vauban was ordered to proceed gently. The Council of Thirteen took advantage of the opportunity to request him to postpone the operation, and when Turenne arrived, the allies held Kehl and the Count von Hohenlohe, representing the Emperor, subsidized the people of the town, to excite their wrath against us. Meeting misfortune with a stout heart, Turenne, to make sure of the advantage of a revulsion of opinion, pretended to believe that the magistrates must have yielded to the people, and he met the situation by other means.

It was a very delicate situation, for the allies, who were much superior in number, lay between the Ill and the Rhine, and cut the French off from Upper Alsace. Luckily they decided to await the Great Elector, who was on his way to join them, crossing the Ill, in order, as they thought, to frighten Turenne; they scattered their corps and were guilty of the blunder of not occupying the fords of the Bruche which might have protected them.

Turenne, being fully resolved to attack them before their junction with the Brandenburgers, seized the opportunity offered him. To reach the enemy, he had to risk a flank march and to cross four streams in succession. He started at midnight on October 2, preceded by several detachments. On the 3d, between three and four in the morning, the detachment of Le Repaire discovered the enemy. Turenne halted the army, then galloped up and made his reconnaissance. He sent an advance-guard, which crossed the stream and occupied a village beyond the last one, the Bruche. He rejoined his advance-guard, inspected the battlefield, and, during the night of October 3–4, led the bulk of his army across and drew it up in battle order on both sides of the bridgehead he had built for himself.

The enemy, having been duly warned, made his dispositions with his center at Ensheim. Rain and a light mist favored Turenne; at his right was a small wood, not occupied; he threw troops into this position, of which the enemy then grasped the importance and for which they fought desperately. On his left Lorge attacked and thus forced the enemy's center and right to engage. At the end of the day the little wood remained in the hands of the French; the allies' right was driven back. Turenne's artillery fire was like a blast from hell; twenty-five hundred shots were fired — a tremendous figure in those days. At nightfall the enemy left the field of battle to an adversary hardly more than half his strength and withdrew behind the Ill. That was manifestly the best place to await the Great Elector.

The maneuvering of the army, and the battle of Ensheim which resulted from it, cannot be too highly praised. Under the conditions in which Turenne found himself, an ordinary general, considering all the elements of his inferiority, would have temporized; the nearness of winter and the King's instructions might have relieved him from responsibility and even have justified in his own eyes a commonplace performance. Turenne, who knew that success can come only by battle, determined to overtake the enemy and whip him. The enemy, although the stronger, had been trying to escape ever since Sinzheim, and for more than four months he succeeded. But on the day when, hesitating, poorly posted, poorly protected, with the junction still incomplete, he slipped within reach of the claw of 'the old fox,' the old fox was on the spot. His technique is not less worthy of admiration, for his audacious decision was carried out with the maximum of prudence: he made sure of an eventual line of retreat in case he should be defeated; he made his dispositions in such a way that he could always meet any danger which might take him by surprise in the course of his maneuvers. He gave proof of remarkable physical endurance and activity; he was always where he was needed, when he was needed, to reckon up the situation for himself and decide. Thanks to all of which, he fought this battle to victory — 'one of the longest, most obstinate and most *artilleryized* that have ever been seen,' to quote the Duc de Bournonville, who knew what he was talking about.

It was high time to strike this blow, for the Great Elector was approaching by rapid marches. Far from slowing him up, the defeat of his allies had redoubled his ardor for a combat which he expected to win easily. 'It won't last long,' he said, encouraged by Bournonville, who wrote: 'M. de Turenne will be compelled to give up all of Alsace to us, and Your Electoral Highness will be able to say, like Cæsar: *Veni, vidi, vici.*' On October 10, he reached Kehl with twenty thousand men and thirty-two guns, and crossed the

Rhine, thus raising the number of the allied forces to fifty-seven thousand. The next day Turenne fell back within range of his two forts, Saverne and Haguenau, declining to fight pending the arrival of the considerable reënforcements he expected to receive. There was grave apprehension at Court, and Louvois, while issuing orders to send the reënforcements, could think of nothing but 'predicting all the dire things that might happen to M. de Turenne.' But the Marshal had told the King that it was necessary that the end of the campaign should not find the enemy on the west side of the Rhine, and he pursued his object without allowing himself to be diverted from it for a moment. From October 30 to November 4, he received the last of the reënforcements, which increased his force to thirty-three thousand men. On November 20, he fell back again, and the allies, already revivified by the news of their own reënforcements and persuaded that Turenne was going into winter quarters, decided to do likewise. They settled down comfortably over a wide expanse in fertile Upper Alsace.

This was the moment Turenne had been waiting for to put in execution a plan long since matured. As early as the month of April, when it was a matter of protecting Franche-Comté, he had conceived and suggested to Louvois the idea

224

of a movement under cover of the mountains, to attack by surprise an enemy force marching through Alsace; but up to that time conditions had not lent themselves to the carrying out of his plan. In November, it was a very different matter, and on the 9th the Marshal wrote to Le Tellier, Louvois being ill at the time: 'In the present condition of affairs the enemy cannot get into Comté unless I have been repulsed. As to Upper Alsace, we have only to drive him out of it if he tries to fix his quarters there, and find out the best road by which to get at him, and that is why I have written to Nancy for grain. If he tries to settle down in Alsace, we leave Saverne and Haguenau well provisioned and march against him over the mountains of Lorraine straight into Upper Alsace.'

As his enemy proceeded to settle down in winter quarters, his purpose became more definite: 'As I cannot afford to leave Haguenau unprotected far in my rear, I am leaving six battalions there and three at Saverne, and I propose to march, as I wrote you, across the mountains of Lorraine to find the easiest place for a descent into Alsace. I shall leave some men at Petite-Pierre.' At last, on December 4, the enemy having definitively gone into winter quarters, the moment for action had arrived. 'I am on my way, leaving the mountains of Lorraine on my left, to inspect the places near Remiremont or a little beyond, to see where I can most easily go down into Alsace.'

We can see from these brief extracts how the first inspiration was born, how it grew into a definite plan when circumstances became favorable, how the success of the plan was made possible by a careful and painstaking preparation, comprising the occupation of Saverne and Petite-Pierre, which would at the same time further Turenne's main movement and make it possible for him to retrace his steps if it should become necessary; the arrangements for supplies would assure the feeding and upkeep of his troops during the long march they would have to undergo.

On December 5, Turenne's army broke camp and started through the snow toward Épinal. On the 12th, it drove detachments of Lorrainers from Épinal and Remiremont. On the 18th, Turenne decided to enter Alsace through Belfort, 'the only place of sufficient size.' The snow was followed by a hard frost. On the 27th, he arrived in the neighborhood of Belfort. At Court his movements were followed with anxiety, and those who prophesied, some months before, the voluntary retreat of the whole army in Lorraine, took alarm and criticized the present abandonment of Alsace, which was, however, only a feint.

Turenne knew all about it; even in his own army there were malcontents, for he had not revealed his intentions. One day, when he was riding with the Chevalier de la Fare, who was his warm friend, he asked him how he thought the campaign would end. La Fare having told him what he thought, Turenne rejoined enigmatically at first: 'The Court is sometimes satisfied when it should not be, and is not satisfied when it should be. For myself, I am doing the best that I believe I can do.' Then he proceeded to reveal his meaning and his hopes in a sentence which will remain true as long as France exists: *'Believe me; there must never be a fighting man at rest in France so long as there is a German on this side of the Rhine in Alsace.'*

Turenne's arrival at Belfort threw the enemy into the greatest confusion. On December 29, he attacked Mülhausen with an advance-guard, which fought a successful battle in the outskirts of the town and drove Bournonville from his headquarters. He sent detachments in all directions in pursuit of the enemy's troops, as they fled northward in hot haste. Then he marched upon Colmar. The allies had taken up a position behind the Logelbach between Colmar and Turkheim, and seemed willing to accept battle; they had occupied Colmar in great strength, but thought it useless to defend Turkheim, which they considered inaccessible. Turenne thought otherwise; arriving on the 4th within striking distance of his adversary, he at once inspected the ground, saw the enemy's error, and decided upon his course accordingly. The next day, January 5, he drew up his forces in three columns; the right and center made a frontal attack; the left marched secretly upon Turkheim through the Val Saint-Grégoire, and occupied in force that commanding point at the very moment that the enemy set out to recapture it. But he was too late, for his forces were immobilized by the frontal attack which enabled Turenne to develop his left-wing maneuver. This maneuver rolled up the enemy's right flank, and during the night he stole away. The magistrates of Strassburg refused to enter into any arrangement with him and thus Turenne reaped the reward of his moderation toward them. Ten days later not a single German was left on the left bank of the Rhine. '*Sexaginta millia Germanorum ultra Rhenum pulsa,*'[1] says the legend of the medal struck in commemoration of the victory of Turkheim. The Duke of Lorraine remarked jestingly that 'Five princes by the grace of God fled before a single prince by the grace of the King of France.'

[1] Sixty thousand Germans driven beyond the Rhine.

Such was this campaign of 1674. Turenne's last — since it was his fate to do no more than begin the following one — and the one in which he rose to the greatest heights.

Since the preceding year the theater of his operations had been broadened tremendously: the region now under his command extended from the Moselle to Switzerland — an immense territory, over which, less than forty years before, four separate armies had maneuvered, to say nothing of the garrisons of the fortresses whose governors were under the direct orders of the King. Doubtless this was so because the royal projects had grown in scope and the royal authority, by becoming more firmly established, tended to give more unity to all its undertakings. But this was not the only cause, and we can safely assert that, while Turenne was so endowed as to keep pace in capacity with the tasks that were assigned him, his genius, by making this evolution possible, contributed immensely to hasten it.

Now he had reached the point of including in his plans all the territory over which the King's armies were fighting; that is to say, all the eastern boundaries of France. When he estimated the relative importance of the various theaters of operation and advised as to the decisions upon which the safety of the State depended, he gave proof of an infallible judgment and of a character even more resolute and more lofty.

In the execution of his plans he had become more enterprising in proportion as he became more perfect in his profession. He was more daring in proportion to his increase in knowledge. Having to contend with new foes who were always more numerous than he, it was by virtue of his knowledge of the weak points of a coalition and by a constantly offensive strategy that he succeeded. He tried to bring on a battle, but with what skill, what science in maneuvering, what stratagems, and also what a genius for making the most of his opponents' blunders and attacking them at the right moment! When he had come up to them, he gave the battle a personal aspect by his activity and the resources of his wit, which never fell short of what Frederick the Great called 'the *à propos* of M. de Turenne.'

His tactics left nothing to chance; knowledge of the enemy, scrutiny of the terrain, estimating of possibilities — everything was taken into account. There was nothing rigid about these tactics; thrice he attacked an enemy strongly entrenched behind a river, thrice he whipped him, and each time a different way. At Sinzheim he made a frontal attack and profited by his superiority in infantry to capture points of support upon which he based the maneuvers of his cavalry. At Ensheim he came up by a flank march and surprised an enemy who deemed himself secure behind several streams; he had formed his lines in front of him before he had recovered from his surprise, and profited especially by the moral effect thus produced. At Turkheim he made his dispositions for battle at a distance, which enabled him to force the enemy to remain in his front and to defeat him by flank movements conducted secretly and with great vigor.

Finally, while he had reached the highest point of his art, he retained all the qualities of his youth: an incomparable fearlessness which set an irresistible example — at Turkheim he had a third horse shot under him — and an activity which carried the master's eye and will to all points at once.

Napoleon blamed Turenne because, as soon as he had forced his way into Alsace in his winter campaign, he did not march straight on Strassburg before the enemy had a chance to rally, and also because he did not then pursue him without respite. We have already called attention to the difference between the wars of the seventeenth century and the merciless struggles of such conflicts between nations and nations as those of the Revolution and Empire. Regarding things with our mental outlook, we cannot fail to regret that Turenne's greatest victories were not followed by pursuit; in that respect we must admit that his art was incomplete; it was reserved for Napoleon to crown his work by the overwhelming and definitive completion of his victories. But Turenne was responsible for tremendous strides in the strategy and tactics of his time; although he did not invent the term, he was really the inventor of the oblique order. Frederick the Great made no mistake about it, and this pupil of Voltaire, who urged his officers to study Turenne's last two campaigns, as 'masterpieces of the strategy of his day,' sang in French verse the victory of Turkheim, thus doing double homage to our tongue and to the Marshal's military genius.

> Sans consulter son art, sans craindre les revers,
> Le Germain se sépare avant les froids hivers;
> Il divise son corps, il cantonne en Alsace,
> Il hâte par ses mains le sort qui le menace;
> Tandis qu'il est flatté par la sécurité,
> Que l'Aigle des Césars s'endort en sûreté,
> Turenne se rassemble au revers des montagnes;
> Il les passe, il parait, il fond dans les campagnes,
> Tombe sur Bournonville, enlève ses quartiers,
> De ses soldats épars, il fait des prisonniers,
> Et force le Germain, par cette rude épreuve,
> A passer en courant vers l'autre bord du fleuve.[1]

---

[1] Without studying his art, without fear of defeat, the German divides his force before the cold winter begins; he separates his divisions, he goes into quarters in Alsace, he hastens with his own hands the fate that threatens him. While he soothes himself by

THE LAST OF TURENNE'S CAMPAIGNS

As soon as he learned of the victory, the King wrote to the Marshal: 'I desire you to return to me; I am impatient to see you and tell you with my own lips of the intense satisfaction that your very considerable and important services throughout the campaign and the latest victory you have won over our enemies have given me.'

Turenne, as his custom was, first ensured the well-being of his army for the rest of the winter, then started for Paris. It is told that, no matter how fast he traveled, he found on his road a multitude of people of all ages and all conditions who had assembled to see him. In Champagne, peasants traveled ten leagues to see him pass, 'and the people of that province, being convinced that they were indebted to him for all the comforts and peace they were enjoying, shed tears of joy as they watched him ride by.'

Turenne reached Paris on January 29. He went at once to Saint-Germain. There they gave him a 'sort of triumphal entry,' by order of the King, who had sent a part of his Court to meet him. Louis XIV came down to greet him, and embraced him, saying, 'You have restored a

the sense of security that the Eagle of the Cæsars sleeps in peace, Turenne musters his troops beyond the mountains, he crosses them, he appears, he rushes down into the plain, falls upon Bournonville, takes his headquarters, makes prisoners of his scattered troops, and by this rough experience forces the German soldiers to run at full speed to the other side of the river.

233

lily to my crown.' He took him that evening to the theater and overwhelmed him with his favors.

Contemporaries relate that people stopped in the street to see him pass, and that even the chair-bearers left their work for a moment's glimpse of him; that in church he was immediately surrounded; and that foreign sovereigns requested his portrait. Bussy himself bows to the prevailing wind and writes to his cousin, 'I tell you that I love M. de Turenne as much as I used to hate him; for to tell you the truth, my heart can hold out no longer before such high desert.'

Amidst all this homage and these manifestations he remained the same. 'His modesty has heightened his glory,' says Pellisson. 'Everybody has discovered that he is a little more retiring than he used to be.' Turenne, although impervious to empty renown, was well aware, none the less, of the greatness of his work and felt a profound satisfaction in having freed France from the danger that threatened her. This is what he expressed in very simple terms to his nephew the Cardinal the day after the victory: 'Although I haven't much to say about what has been going on lately, I am fully aware that it has been very fortunate and advantageous to the King's service.'

Indeed, pride was so far removed from him at the moment of his greatest triumph that he thought of retiring to the Oratory. It will be remembered that the King insisted that he should resume command of his army in the spring.

The Marshal had not, however, abandoned this project, and Madame de Sévigné tells us that before setting out he had confided in the Cardinal de Retz, saying to him: 'Monsieur, I am not much of a talker, but I beg you to believe, seriously, that if it were not for this business in which I may be needed I should retire, like you; and I give you my word, that, if I return, I shall not die with my boots on and I shall follow your example in putting some time between life and death.'

But God had decided otherwise.

Chapter VII

THE DEATH OF TURENNE: THE HOMAGE PAID TO HIM BY HIS CONTEMPORARIES AND BY POSTERITY

OPERATIONS began anew in May, 1675. Turenne had at his disposal twenty-five thousand men of the veteran regiments. 'I have never seen so many good men or men better disposed,' he wrote to Louvois immediately on rejoining his army. The Emperor opposed to him Montecuculli, his adversary of 1673, who marched straight upon Strassburg. Turenne hurried thither and prevented him from crossing the Rhine. After this first passage at arms the armies simply watched each other.

The Marshal received from the Court instructions which contained always the same contradictions in terms. For example, in the same letter the King forbade him to cross the Rhine before a fixed date, then gave him leave to do whatever he should consider best adapted to enhance the glory of his army, and ended by recurring to his original restricted orders: 'I doubt not that you will conform to what I have written above as to my purposes, with the punctuality which you owe me.'

Turenne received this message at the most critical moment of this Strassburg affair; he replied to it still in the same sense, for his theory of obedience was well established; but this time the form alone was different and delightful in its poise and its confidence in himself and in his master.

'I think Your Majesty will do me the honor to believe that I shall never disobey you except when, being at a distance, I feel sure that you would take it ill of me and that it would be altogether injurious to your service to do things that you would not order me to do if you were on the spot, and I understand full well that Your Majesty might be angry, and that even success would not justify me, but in that case I shall rely only on Your Majesty's goodness.'

Indeed, never was freedom of initiative more necessary to a commander. Montecuculli, intent above all else upon Strassburg, because it would ensure his crossing of the river and because of the supplies he should find there, tried to deceive his adversary concerning his intentions, and several weeks passed in scientific maneuvers, in which Strassburg was the stake.

At the end of July, Turenne had succeeded in forcing the Imperialists northward, while crowding them against the Rhine. On the 27th, at break of day, he formed his army in battle order

237

near Salzbach, and sent young Saint-Hilaire to
look up favorable positions for the artillery commanded by his father, so that the latter 'could
bring up the guns; for in a short time this may
become a very serious business.' His dispositions
once made, he declared himself satisfied and said
to the Comte de Roze, who was with him: 'Good
enough; it seems to me that this isn't at all bad,
and I think Montecuculli would approve what
we have done.' Then he sat down at the foot of a
tree which he told an old trooper to climb and tell
him what he could see of the enemy. Learning
shortly after that Montecuculli was sending his
baggage-trains over the mountains, he decided
that he was preparing to steal away, and he
wrote to the King that he was disposing his
forces to attack him during that move. At two
in the afternoon, the direction taken by a German column seemed to confirm his judgment
and he ordered M. de Roze to go and overlook
this march. Roze went away, then sent several
messengers to beg the Marshal to come at once
to see for himself what was going on.

He mounted and rode to the right wing of the
army. 'On the way,' says Saint-Hilaire, who
was with him, 'he spied my father, and as he
honored him with his confidence, he rode to
meet him. When he joined him, he asked what
that column was on account of which they had

sent for him. My father was pointing it out to him when, unhappily, two small guns were discharged; one of the shots, passing over the croup of my father's horse, took off his left arm and the top of my brother's horse's neck, and struck M. de Turenne in the left side. He rode some twenty yards on his horse, then fell dead. Thus ends this great man, who never had an equal, and I can affirm that all the details I have given are the exact truth. None of those who have written about him know them as I do.'

They covered the Marshal's body with a cloak, and took it to a tent, in order to keep his death secret, but the army soon knew of the disaster that had befallen it, and a deserter made haste to bear the news to the enemy.

Turenne's troops, angered by the joyful outcry and bursts of music from the hostile camp, would fain have avenged their leader and demanded to be led against the enemy. Nothing had been provided for the succession to the command in case anything happened. Vauban was the senior lieutenant-general, but the Comte de Lorge was officer of the day. In the general confusion it was decided to recross the Rhine. The rear-guard fought a desperate battle in which all showed themselves worthy of their leader. Montecuculli had to abandon the field, with a loss of two thousand troops, a large number of standards, seven cannon, leaving Turenne's army free to withdraw behind the river.

From the very spot where Turenne was stricken, Vauban had written to Louvois to tell him of his death. It was through this letter that the first news reached the King, on July 29. He received it at the moment he was about to sit down at table, only two hours after the last report written by the Marshal. Having read the letter, he heaved a tremendous sigh. It is told also that he said at the moment that he would have preferred to lose two battles or even twenty thousand soldiers.

On the 31st, when Boisguyot reached Paris, from him were learned the details of the circumstances under which Turenne had met his death and the grief of the whole army. This overwhelming news, following after only a few months the triumphal return of January, sorely afflicted all France. 'There is no one in Paris,' said a foreign ambassador, 'who would not gladly give all he owns to bring back to earth a man of such unexampled worth.'

The King bore witness nobly to his esteem for him. Although Turenne had written in his will that he wished to be buried in the parish of the commune in which he died, with as little ceremony as possible, Louis XIV, who knew how to

do honor to those who served him, decided that
he should be buried at Saint-Denis, in the very
chapel of the Bourbons.

The writings and correspondence of contemporaries are filled with tales of the grief of the
Marshal's friends and kindred. Condé wrote to
Louvois of his grief as 'the greatest imaginable.'
The Cardinal de Bouillon, who learned the news
by chance, fainted. Villeroi, La Rochefoucauld,
and the Cardinal de Retz made no secret of
their emotion. Bossuet was so stricken that he
nearly lost consciousness and regained his senses
very slowly. Madame de Sévigné and her circle
were inconsolable; she wrote to her daughter
that a month after their friend's death, she and
Mesdames d'Elbeuf and de La Fayette met and
talked over all the details of his death and wept
together. La Fare, who lived with Turenne
during his last campaign, wrote: 'For my part
I confess that of all the men I ever knew he
seemed to me nearest perfection.' Such homage
lay in the hearts of all Frenchmen. The mourning of the country was universal.

On August 12, after a funeral sermon in camp,
where 'the tears of the soldiers were the genuine
mourning,' the hero's body was taken to Saint-
Denis. Now again there was a great multitude
on the Alsace road, to pay their last respects to

him, but with what different feelings! The people poured forth from town and village to receive the body, and the clergy accompanied it from place to place. At Langres the ceremonies, in which the people took part, were particularly stately and solemn. The melancholy journey was made slowly amid public manifestations of grief. It came to an end on August 29. It was ten o'clock at night when they arrived at Saint-Denis. Eight of M. de Turenne's Guard lifted the body from the funeral car. The Prior came out to receive it, with M. Boucherat; then the guards bore it into the choir where the prayers customary on such occasions were read. It was a melancholy ceremony; M. Boucherat, who was looking on, 'thought that he should die of weeping.' The same night Turenne's heart was taken to the Carmelite Convent.

The next day the monks of Saint-Denis celebrated a service at which only the family, the servants, and a small number of friends were present: MM. de Meaux, Boucherat, Harlay, Bouillon, Mmes. de Sévigné, d'Elbeuf, and Boucherat. And finally, Louis XIV, in order to do homage to Turenne more publicly and solemnly, ordered that 'a service should be celebrated in his name on September 9, at Notre Dame, to pray to Almighty God for the soul of the most noble, generous, and puissant lord

Prince Henri de La Tour d'Auvergne, Vicomte de Turenne, Maréchal-Général of the King's Camps and Armies and Colonel-General of the Light Cavalry, who was killed by a cannon-shot on July 27 near Salzbach, while reconnoitering the enemy's position on the eve of attacking him.' The Bishop of Lombez delivered the panegyric of the Marshal.

This official demonstration did not stand by itself. Every one, at Court, in the city, and among the common people, talked of Turenne, citing incidents of his life; the better they came to know him, the more, it seemed, they admired him. Everywhere it was regarded as a duty to do honor to his memory. At the opening of the Parliament of Paris, Lamoignon eulogized the grandeur of that famous man, 'the terror of the Empire and Spain, the adoration of his soldiers, and the admiration of all Europe.' At the Carmelites, in October, Mascaron 'described him truly, with his great heart, his uprightness, and the ingenuousness of spirit in which he was moulded.' And in January, 1676, at Saint-Eustache, Fléchier delivered the last funeral oration. These services and these addresses kept public sorrow alive for months. Then came silence, but not oblivion.

All those of Turenne's contemporaries who

left journals, memoirs, or letters, mentioned him. These documents, brought to light one after another, have constantly revived interest in his personality. That is why he continued to fill so large a place in the eighteenth century, not in the memory of French generals, who, however, would have gained so much by meditating upon his acts and his writings, but in the reflections of the most cultivated men. Many of them studied the life of Turenne and became intensely interested in some of the problems that it presented. Thus Voltaire and President Hénault discussed the sincerity of his conversion. Voltaire, by the way, took a deep interest in Turenne; although he knew nothing of his letters or of the part he played in diplomacy, he strove to force his way through the panegyrics to the real man; he studied his quarrels with Louvois, he disclosed his weaknesses and his faults — 'which were common to him and so many other men' — with excessive harshness, perhaps; but he concluded that his virtues and his great talents, which were unique, should cause everything else to be forgotten. Finally, one day when, irritated no doubt by the monotonous eulogiums, he had enumerated all that he could find to blame him for, he wrote in conclusion: 'Notwithstanding all this, I think he was one of the greatest men we have ever had'; which was no slight praise from his pen.

Jean-Jacques Rousseau, above all the rest, sought in Turenne's life passages likely to stir his emotions. The philosophers were led to admire his kindness to his subordinates and to all little ones; and D'Argenson declared that he 'was equally mourned by soldiers and people — praise which no general had earned since the glorious days of the Roman Republic and Empire.'

This inflated style is almost that of the Revolution, the leaders of which expressed a similar judgment of Turenne. He was, in truth, the only one of the prominent men of the old régime who escaped their hatred, and they did honor to his memory in a very special way. After the violation of the tombs at Saint-Denis in 1793, Turenne's body was preserved at the Museum. In 1796, a member of the Council of Five Hundred moved in the Assembly that the Directory be requested to deposit those august remains in a more respectable place. Turenne, he said in the jargon of the place, 'lived under a King, but it was the error of the period and not a crime on that hero's part; his prejudices were those of the times in which he lived; his virtues were his own.' His motion was adopted unanimously; but it had no sequel until three years later, when Turenne's remains were deposited in the Musée des Monuments Français, in the former cloister of the Petits Augustins.

It was reserved for the first captain of modern times to render the last honors to him whom he regarded as the greatest general of the monarchy. Bonaparte, the First Consul, decided that Turenne's body should be taken to the Invalides, to the mausoleum originally built at Saint-Denis, which had escaped destruction. The ceremony took place September 22, 1800, the day of the celebration of the anniversary of the Republic. At the same time with the hero of times past, they also did homage to the first Grenadier of France, La Tour d'Auvergne, who fell in the Army of the Rhine, and Kléber, who was murdered in Egypt. It was a very solemn occasion; before the Marshal's body was laid the sword that he wore at Salzbach and the ball that struck him. Lazare Carnot, after recalling in most eloquent terms what the man and the warrior had been, ended with these words, which deeply moved the multitude of spectators: 'What can I say of Turenne? Behold the man himself. Of his triumphs? Here is the sword held by his victorious arm. Of his death? Here is the fatal ball that stole him from France and all mankind.'

In that tomb he still rests. The pedestal, surrounded by figures of Valor and Wisdom, bore a few years ago the phrase remembered by La Fare: 'There must not be a soldier at rest in

246

France so long as there is a German in Alsace.'
Since the late war the inscription has disappeared; it has been decided, no doubt, that it has
become meaningless.

Turenne's heart had been transferred by the
Cardinal de Bouillon from the chapel of the
Carmelites to the abbatial church of Cluny.
Being saved in the revolutionary tumults and
preserved by the municipality of Cluny, it was
restored to the Marshal's family in 1818.

Like the French themselves, the enemies of
France paid to Turenne the tribute of their
admiration. On learning of his end, Montecuculli said: 'There has died to-day a man who
did honor to mankind.' More than a hundred
years later, in 1814, General Ermolof, commanding the Second Russian Division of the Guard,
which was passing through Salzbach on its way
to fight against France, led his regiments past
the monument which the Cardinal de Rohan had
erected there. He stood beside the leafless tree
preserved by the veneration of the inhabitants.
His regiments came to a halt and at a sign from
him the troops gave three hurrahs — a salute to
the Great Captain on foreign territory.

CONCLUSION

Turenne had hardly disappeared when he became a legendary figure. Everything tended to this result: his simple life, his unusual reserve, which surrounded him like a sort of veil; the nature and extent of his services, which gave him universal renown; and his glorious death which, following so closely upon his most dazzling triumphs, gave him no time to decline in glory and his contemporaries no time to forget him. He ended in an apotheosis.

This legend of Turenne, collected, embellished, and perpetuated by eulogists in the pay of the Bouillon family, has transmitted to the following generations a washed-out figure in the tones of an untarnished and monotonous virtue, whose characteristic features are woefully besmirched. It was that Turenne, no doubt, whom Montesquieu knew and of whom he was thinking when he wrote with admiration shadowed by a regret and a smile: 'Turenne had no vices; perhaps if he had had some, he would have carried certain virtures further. His life is a hymn in praise of mankind.'

If Montesquieu could return to earth and see Turenne, as we can, in the broad daylight of historic truth, he would be content to discern in him, not vices, but passions, by virtue of which he became a man and not a theoretical and abstract hero of legend. He would have concluded, as we have, that, far from losing by being known as he was, he appears quite as good but more alive and more original, with qualities and a mode of life quite individual and virtues which he carried as far as possible.

What strikes one at first in Turenne is the perfect harmony of his faculties, which made him a man of unusually well-balanced mind. His intelligence did not go forward by sudden flashes, but as it was susceptible of 'extraordinary application,' as it was guided by an infallible judgment and by an acute perception of reality, everything that it gave forth, in counsel as well as in military command, was sensible and practical. 'The unique sum-total of all the greatness of this incomparable hero, in my opinion,' as the Abbé du Plessis has very happily put it, 'is that he was a hero with the aid of common-sense, a hero of cool judgment without excitement or impulsiveness, and always in accord with reason.' Thanks to this genial common-sense of his, he built on the rock, and in whatever domain he was called upon to exert his activity, political or diplomatic, as well as military, his outlook was always well-founded and virile.

This intellectual robustness became in due time the most powerful stay of his character. He could make up his mind, because he knew; he could persist in what he made up his mind to do, because he had meditated long over his decision and for him it had taken on the semblance of truth. Hence, his exceptional moral courage and strength of character.

Now, equilibrium between talents and character is the very thing which, in Napoleon's opinion, makes great generals. 'The thing which was most desirable,' he said at Saint Helena, 'and would at once raise a man above the ruck, was that in him the mind should be in equilibrium with his character.' That is what he called being 'as square at the top as at the bottom.' These words apply admirably to Turenne. Perhaps Napoleon may have been thinking that day of him of whom he said elsewhere: 'Of all the generals who have gone before me and will perhaps come after me, the greatest is Turenne.'

In Turenne, in very truth, his military talents were quite on a level with his character. He knew the value of moral forces and he handled them in a masterly way. In strategy, as in tactics, he introduced an innovation in that he advocated constant movement and battles in an age when only a war of sieges was held in honor; that he attributed chief importance to artillery fire;

that he skillfully combined movement with the use of entrenchments; and that he did everything with a sense of what was happening always on the alert and with incredible resources for 'putting right something that had gone wrong.' Most of the rules that he acted upon would still find their application in our day.

And doubtless he would have had his school of followers if some one of his contemporaries had extracted from his Memoirs, his instructions, his correspondence, and from conversations with him, the principles by whose application he led his armies to victory; but nothing of the sort happened. Turenne's teachings were therefore lost to France down to the day when Napoleon unearthed them and gave them his sanction. On the other hand, they were, as we have seen, followed in other lands. Often, indeed, after a successful war the victor has fallen asleep in a fallacious assurance of his superiority, while his opponent, striving to work out the causes of his defeat, struggles to recover from it. Hence, the victor of to-day becomes the vanquished of to-morrow: Rossbach succeeds Turkheim; Sedan, Jena; Rethondes, Sedan; may we not forget it!

With knowledge Turenne combined the prestige indispensable to a general to enable him to lead his soldiers to great deeds. People may think — erroneously in our opinion — that in national armies, where love of country keeps the soldier to his duty and spurs him on to the most heroic deeds, the ascendancy of the commander has become of less importance; but in the armies of the old régime, which comprised only mercenary troops and a large proportion of foreigners, it was unquestionably necessary that the leader should be an inspirer of men. Turenne's prestige was made up of several elements. His soldiers were aware of his valor, they were proud to follow a general who led them always to victory. They knew him to be sparing of shedding their blood, sympathetic with their hardships, and overflowing with generosity. In a word, they saw him amongst them teaching by example, sharing their perils and their fatigues, exposing himself always in the front rank.

There was, then, in Turenne, a marvelous balancing of the high qualities which it is uncommon to find in the same man.

Another trait impressed all who knew him — his simplicity — the amazing simplicity of his mode of life, of his greeting, of his manners, placed in even stronger relief by contrast with the suspicious pride that he manifested as soon as there was any question of the rank of his family.

With this outward simplicity was allied the

inward quality that is its complement — sincerity. He was always true with himself and never sought to shine under false appearances. And this quality had important consequences.

The first is that, having no part to learn, he found time and acquired a taste for meditation and for the inward life; hence his convictions sank deeper just as his 'obscurities' also increased as regards those who could not follow the working of his mind.

The second consequence is that he remained to an eminent degree capable of attaining greater heights. In his youth he had not sought to shine, but merely to learn. Throughout his life it was the same. As he was not the slave of a character which he wished to enact, he was capable of transforming himself into a different personality by the constant keeping-up of the treasures of his intellectual and moral acquirements.

And so — and it may be that this was the most characteristic feature of that noble life — Turenne never ceased to rise higher. As he grew older, his faculties flowered with greater power and originality. His last years, like his last campaign, were the finest. His outlook broadened as his functions increased in importance. His character rose higher and became stronger. At the same time — for all things are connected

— the love and veneration that his troops felt for him became greater to the very end of his life. 'The only general whose audacity grew with years and experience!' said Napoleon, after Bussy had observed that 'Turenne's patience was due to his temperament, and his audacity to his experience.' This life, never declining, but becoming greater and nobler as it passed, makes one think of a great river which grows broader and broader as it goes from its source to end in a limitless bay whose majestic expanse the eyes contemplate with wonder.

If, to conclude, one turns from the noble spectacle of this life to look at the man, we find him always simple in manner, generous, loyal to his friends, and of an incredible modesty. We recall that when La Bruyère wished to depict true grandeur, it was Turenne whom he chose for his portrait: 'True grandeur is free-mannered, gentle, familiar, popular; it allows itself to be touched and handled; it can lose nothing by being seen near at hand; the better one knows it, the more one admires it; it stoops in kindliness to its inferiors and rises without effort to its natural stature.' And we have the secret of the unique sentiment which he aroused in the men of his time in whom affection was blended with admiration.

At Cluny, where Turenne's heart was pre-

CONCLUSION

served for nearly one hundred and fifty years, the old men at the beginning of the nineteenth century used to tell the following anecdote: Two grenadiers who had served under Turenne, and who stopped at the abbey in the early years of the eighteenth century, asked to see their general's heart. Their request was granted gladly: whereupon they drew their sabers and held them crosswise over that relic; then they knelt and said a short prayer with tears in their eyes.

This touching act of homage is a symbol of that which posterity has paid, not only to Turenne's genius, but to his great heart.

THE END

INDEX

Throughout the index *T.* stands for the subject of the study.

257

INDEX

Arnauld, Antoine ('Arnauld the Great'), influence on *T.* of his writings on the Eucharist, 177; and *T.*'s conversion, 186

Arras, attack on besiegers of, after fall of Stenay, 74; besieged by Condé and Spaniards, 72 ff.; *T.*'s activity, 73; his difficulties from lack of everything, 73, 74; siege of, raised by *T.* after fierce battle, 74–76; victory of, raised *T.*'s fame to highest point, 77

Artillery dates only from Louvois, 17

Aumont, Maréchal d', and *T.*'s right to give orders, 158; mentioned, 83, 154

Austria, France aims to hold in check, 124

Auvergne, Comte d', *T.*'s nephew, marries a Hohenzollern, 101

Avaux, M. d', letter of Mazarin to, 37, 38

Baas, M. de, 81

Barillon, Marquis de Morangis, tries to convert Mme. de Turenne, 173

Bassecourt, M. de, 91

Bavaria, Duke of. *See* Maximilian.

Bavaria, invaded by *T.*, 48, 49

Bellefonds, Maréchal de, refuses to serve under *T.*, exiled, and submits, 191, 192

Blumenthal, Herr von, 128

Boisguyot, M. de, 139

Bois-le-Duc, *T.*'s first military experience at (1629), 11, 12

Bonn, captured by the allies, 206

Bork, M., *T.*'s agent in Berlin, 128

Bossuet, Jacques Bénigne, influence of, on *T.*, 178; his *Exposition of the Catholic Faith*, 179, 180; mentioned, 241

Boucherat, M. de, 135, 136, 144, 242

Boucherat, Mme. de, 242

Bouillon, Cardinal de, 208, 234, 241, 242, 247. *And see* Albret, Duc d'

Bouillon, Duc de, I, *T.*'s father. *See* La Tour d'Auvergne, Henri

Bouillon, Duc de, II, *T.*'s oldest brother by his father's second wife, Elizabeth of Nassau, inherits his father's ambition and love of intrigue, 26; influence of his Catholic wife converts him to Catholicism, 26, 27; gives Soissons shelter at Sedan and refuses to surrender him, 28; treats with the Emperor and makes Sedan once more the center of intrigue, 27, 28; after death of Soissons, obtains his pardon and restoration of his estates and privileges, 28; involved in conspiracy of Cinq-Mars, but is again pardoned, 28, 29; new plots of, in Spain, 54; still among the malcontents, 56; confirmed in his title of sovereign prince, 61; death of, and *T.*'s grief, 65; his conversion did not move *T.*, 168; his last will, 168; mentioned, 4, 9, 35, 36, 53, 55

Bouillon, Duchesse de. *See* La Mark, Charlotte de

Bouillon, Duchesse de, II (Elizabeth of Nassau), *T.*'s mother, her treaty with Richelieu in 1629 results in *T.*'s being sent to serve in France as hostage for fulfilment of her pledges, 3, 4; an ardent Calvinist, 9; left with 2 sons and 5 daughters, 9; sends her sons to Holland, to be trained in arms under her brothers Maurice and Frederick Henry of Nassau, 9; letter of *T.* to, concerning his brother, 27, 28, 29;

INDEX

dies from shock at surrender of Sedan, 29; mentioned, 7, 11, 20, 50, 166, 167, 171

Bouillon, Duchesse de, III, T.'s sister-in-law, plots against France at Brussels, 54; her death, 175

Bouillon, Mme. de, T.'s niece by marriage, 142

Bouillon, Duchy of, one of the 'Sovereign States,' 4

Bouillon, House of, T. always placed its interest above all else, 4; substituted for that of La Mark in possession of 'Sovereign States,' 7; once more rehabilitated after Peace of Reuil, 56; its affairs settled satisfactorily to T., 68; preponderant influence of, 100 ff.; its connection with foreign princely families, 100, 101; European in the true sense, 101; religious unity of, no longer unimpaired, 103; T.'s devotion to, rights and privileges of, 133; not wealthy, 135

Bouillons and Le Telliers, rivalry between. See Le Telliers

Bournonville, Duc de, 220, 222, 223, 227

Brandenburg, Elector of. See Frederick William, the Great Elector

Brandenburg, Electorate of, T.'s prevision of future greatness of, 129

Breda, Treaty of, 131

Brienne, 168

Brisach, captured by T. in campaign of 1638, 24

Brussels, 92

Bussy, Maréchal de, 143

Bussy-Rabutin, Roger de, quoted, 13, 85, 86, 134, 189, 234

Campaign of 1658, brevity of, 161, 162, 163

Campaign of 1667, a complete success for T., 156; had he reason to be wholly satisfied with? 156 ff.

Campaign of 1672, called a military promenade, 194, but marks the beginning of a new régime, 194

Campaign of 1673 on the Rhine, a difficult one for T., 203; reënforcements refused him, 203

Campaign of 1674, 213 ff.

Carmelites, Convent of, 147

Carnot, Lazare, quoted on T., 246

Casale, Mazarin and T. began their careers before walls of, 20

Castelnau, General, joins T. before Dunkirk, 83; his death a calamity, 87

Catalonia, 16

Catherine, Infanta of Portugal, marries Charles II of England, 124, 125

Caumont, Charlotte de, marries T., 61 and n.; the marriage strengthens his Protestant ties, 168. And see Turenne, Mme. de

Cavalry, the status and methods of, in early 17th century, 17; importance of brigadiers in, 115

Chalais, Comte de, 15

Châtillon, Duchesse de, 97

Chédigny, M. de, 187

Cherasco, Treaty of, negotiated by Mazarin, 20

Chevreuse, Duchesse de, 95

Choisel, Gilbert de, Bishop, 176

Choisy, M. de, quoted, 147, 166, 176, 184, 186

Charles I of England, 78

Charles II of England, marries the Infanta Catherine of Braganza, 124; and T., 125, 126, 163, 164; mentioned, 101, 102 and n., 130, 176

Charles, Infante of Spain, afterward Charles II, 130

259

INDEX

Cinq-Mars, Henri de, Bouillon involved in conspiracy of, 28, 29; executed with de Thou, 29

Claude, minister, 177, 178

Clement IX, Pope, and *T.*'s conversion, 182; offers cardinalate to *T.*, 185

Clerville, Major General de, at Mardyck, 82

Cluny, incident at, 254, 255

Coalition forces against French, numerical supremacy of, 229; misunderstandings between, 219, 220; decide to march on Strassburg, 220, but to await arrival of the Great Elector, 221; beaten by *T.* at Ensheim, 221, 222; driven east of the Rhine, 228

Coatquen, Mme. de, result of *T.*'s attraction to, 148

Colbert, Jean-Baptiste, and *T.*, 111; acts as Mazarin's private secretary during the Fronde, 111 *n.*; eventually at head of every department, except war, 111 *n.*, 112; his economical turn runs counter to *T.*'s demand for experienced and disciplined officers, 159; favors making peace with the Triple Alliance, 162; mentioned, 123, 125, 140, 146, 160

Colbert de Croissy, at London, *T.* drafts instructions for, 163, 164

Colbert du Terron, Intendant, 125

Colmar, 227

Cologne, Elector of, 131

Colonel-General of Cavalry, importance of post, 112

Concini, Concino, Marquis d'Ancre, 8 and *n.*, 53

Condé, Henri II de, 8 *n.*

Condé, Louis, Prince de (Louis I de Bourbon, father of the great Condé), and Concini, 53

Condé, Louis II, Prince de (Louis II de Bourbon, known as the Duc d'Enghien before his father's death), the great Condé, with the Army of Germany at Fribourg, quoted on *T.*, 40; takes over command of Army of Germany and whips General Mercy at Nordlingen, 42; again commends *T.*, 42; illness compels him to leave the army, 43; letter of *T.* to, 55, 56; *T.* pays a visit to, 56; arrested and committed to Vincennes for conspiring against Mazarin, 57; *T.* refuses to abandon him, 57; set free, 59; his letter of affection and gratitude to *T.*, 60; revolts again at Guyenne and parleys with Spain (1652), 62; attacks d'Hocquincourt at Gien and is beaten, 63; *T.*'s opinion of, as an opponent, 70; lays siege to Arras, 72 ff.; at Arras, defeats La Ferté and is driven off by *T.*, 76; his cordiality to Cromwell, 78; learns of movement from Dunkirk and rides to meet it, 86, 87; pardoned by Louis XIV, 92; letter of Mazarin to *T.* on Condé's return to France, 96, 97; *T.*'s relations with, 143; quoted, on *T.*, 151, 152; *T.*'s remarks to, on the general conduct of war, 157; *T.* long aware of the purpose to place him at head of the army, 161; effect of his being so placed on *T.*'s enemies, 161; favors fighting the Triple Alliance, 162; in war with Holland, 195; in campaign of 1674, 213, 214; in Flanders, 217 ff.; Louis XIV wishes *T.* to send reënforcements to, 218; result of his victory at Seneffe, 219; quoted, on *T.*'s death, 241; mentioned, 49, 50, 55, 78, 98, 109, 110, 115

INDEX

Conti, Armand de Bourbon, Prince de, 57

Conti, Prince de, and Longueville, Marquis de, on *T*.'s entry into France with Spanish troops, to free them, had to be removed from Vincennes, 59; set free by Mazarin, 59

Conti, Mme. de, 179

Corsican Guard, affair of the, settled by *T*., 129

Council of State, a, conjectures as to Louis the XIV's purpose with regard to, after Mazarin's death, 98, 99

Councils, how constituted after Mazarin's death, 109, 110

Court, grave apprehension at, after Ensheim, 224

Créqui, Maréchal Duc de, dissatisfaction with the mission intrusted to him, 158; refuses to serve under *T*., exiled, and submits, 192; mentioned, 129, 154, 155

Cromwell, Oliver, leaned at first toward Spain, and why, 78; and Condé, 78; finally deals with Mazarin, 78, 79; his haste to have possession of Dunkirk, 79, 80; mentioned, 82, 102 *n*.

Cromwell, Richard, 102 *n*.

De Witt, Cornelius, murdered, 196

De Witt, Jan, Grand Pensionary, *T*. supports, in negotiations with Holland, 127; murdered, 196

Denmark, alliance between France and, 128

Depredations by victorious troops, upheld by political morality of the time, 205

Desroziers, *T*.'s maître d'hôtel, 187

Devolution, law of, 130

Devolution, War of. *See* War

Du Boc, Protestant minister, *T*. obtains his pardon, 172

Duhan de Janden, *T*.'s secretary, 139

Dunes, battle of the. *See* Dunkirk

Dunkirk, in Treaty of Paris, 79; Cromwell's haste to get possession of, 79; *T*. comes under walls of, 83 ff.; *T*. decides to march to meet the enemy, 85 ff.; Spaniards and Condé driven away from, 87, 88; celebration of the victory, 88; Napoleon quoted in his *Précis*, etc., 89, 90; fall of (1658), 91; restored to France, 126

Duras, Duchesse de, *T*.'s third sister, 101, 167

Dutlingen, battle of, 36, 37

Dykes, opening of, 83

Elbeuf, Duc d' (Charles III of the House of Lorraine), marries *T*.'s niece, 101

Elbeuf, Mme. d', *T*.'s niece, 142, 241, 242

Eleonore of Bergues marries the Duc de Bouillon (*T*.'s brother), 26; a Catholic, 26, 27; converts her husband, 27. *And see* Bouillon, Duchesse de, III

Elizabeth of Nassau (daughter of William, Prince of Orange), second wife of Henri de La Tour d'Auvergne, and *T*.'s mother. *See* Bouillon, Duchesse de, II

Enghien, Duc d'. *See* Condé, Prince de (Louis II de Bourbon)

Enghien, Duc d', son of the great Condé, 195

Engineering, not known until Vauban, 17

England, France finds it hard to keep peace between Holland and, 123; *T*.'s status in, 125–27; and the affair of the flag, 126; *T*.

INDEX

XIII, Queen-Dowager of England, 95

Herwarth, M., banker, 55, 56

Hesse-Cassel, Landgrave of, 101

High Command and government, proper relations between, 209–12

Hocquincourt, Maréchal d', given command of half the army, 62; attacked by Condé, 63; with T.'s aid, defeats Condé, 63; divides authority with T., 74; at Arras, 76; negotiates with Spaniards, 77; T. saves, from effect of his treachery, 77; rebellion of, 83; killed before Dunkirk, 84; mentioned, 64

Holland, T. definitively quits service of, 21; plan to put T. at head of all troops of, 123; T. has large part in negotiation of treaty of commerce with, 127, 128; attitude of, toward French invasion of Flanders, 160; war with, 190 ff.; dykes cut by the Dutch, 196. *And see* England, Triple Alliance.

Huguenots, T.'s affection for, 174; and Jansenists, 176. *And see* Protestants

Humières, Maréchal d', refuses to serve under T., is exiled, and submits, 191, 192; mentioned, 85, 137

Infantry, how armed, 17

Inn, River, 'T. the first French general to plant the national colors on banks of' (Napoleon), 49

Invalides, Napoleon orders T.'s body transferred to, 246

Jansenists, Huguenots and, 176; influence of, on T.'s conversion, 177

Juan, Don, of Spain, at Dunkirk, 87

Kléber, Jean-Baptiste, 246

La Bruyère, Jean de, 254

La Capelle, taken by T., 78

La Fare, Chevalier de, 227, 241, 246

La Fayette, Mme. de, 147, 241

La Ferté, Maréchal de, divides authority with T., 74; at Arras, 74; taken prisoner by Condé, 78; mentioned, 141

La Fontaine, Jean de, T.'s friendship with, 144; a loyal adherent of the House of Bouillon, 145

La Force, Henri N. de Caumont, Duc de, 21, 168

La Herse, Vialart de, Bishop of Châlons, 176

La Mark, Charlotte de, heiress of the 'Sovereign States,' marries Henri de La Tour d' Auvergne, 5; terms of her inheritance, 5; dies childless, 6

La Meilleraye, Maréchal de, 99

La Mesnadière, quoted, 91

La Motte, T. distinguishes himself at siege of, 21

La Moussaie, M. de, governor of Stenay, 57

La Moussaye, Marquise de, T.'s sister, 101

La Rochefoucauld, M. de, 241

La Rochefoucauld, Comtesse de, T.'s sister, 101

La Rochelle, Assembly of, 8

La Rochelle, Peace of, forced upon the Protestants by Richelieu (1628), 15 and *n.*

La Tour d'Auvergne, the first Grenadier of France, 246

La Tour d'Auvergne, Charlotte de, T.'s only unmarried sister, her *petit nom*, 12; letters of T. to, 35, 42; T.'s confidante, never married, 101; her Protestant ardor, 167

La Tour d'Auvergne, Fébronie de, T.'s niece, her hand refused by Don Pedro of Portugal, 125; mar-

264

INDEX

Parliament of Paris, declaring war on Mazarin, appeals to the King, 52; incites citizens to take up arms and expel the Court, which retires to Saint-Germain, 55; authorizes the return of *T.*'s troops to Paris, 56; how *T.*'s purpose was foiled, 58

Pascal, Blaise, 175

Patriotism, not a definite conception in *T.*'s time, 51

Peace of the Church, may have been what finally brought about *T.*'s conversion, 180 and *n.*

Peace of Clement IX. *See* Peace of the Church

Peace of Reuil, results of, 56

Peace of Ulm, Duke of Bavaria forced to accept, 46

Pedro, Dom, 125

Pellisson, Paul, quoted, 234

Pertuis, M., 88, 139

Philip IV of Spain, *T.* negotiates treaty with, 58; quoted on *T.*, 95; French claim the Low Countries on his death without children by his first wife, 130; mentioned, 73

Plessis, Abbé du, 249

Plessis, Maréchal du, 66

Plessis-Mornay, M. du, *T.* reads his memoirs, 169; the impression they made on him, 169

Plessis-Praslin, Maréchal Duc de, defeats *T.* at Rethel, 59; mentioned, 110, 158

Podevils, Colonel, *T.*'s agent in Berlin, 128

Port-Royal, attraction of, for *T.*, and influence of, on his conversion, 176–78, 180 *n.*

Portugal, France obliged to cease supporting her openly, 102; continues clandestine support, 103; attitude of Anne of Austria, 103; *T.* plays chief part in support

given to, 103, 104; mentioned, 16

Princes, the (Condé, Conti, Longueville), united with Parliament against Mazarin, 62; Mazarin refuses to allow *T.* to attack them in Paris, where they have no troops, 64; *T.* defeats their army at Étampes, 64

Prince Palatine of Bavaria, quoted, 176

Princess Palatine, 75, 147

Protestants, *T.* the moral leader of, by virtue of his rank, 104; his marriage to an ardent Calvinist gave confidence to his coreligionists, 103, 104; anger of, at *T.*'s conversion, 182 ff. *And see* Huguenots

Puysegur, Maréchal de, 143

Pyrenees, treaty of, terms of, 93

'Quarrel of the marshals,' 191–93

Quiers, fight on the road to, 24

Racine, Jean, 167

Rambure, Mme. du, 168

Rantzau, Maréchal de, defeat and capture of, at Dutlingen (1641), a serious set-back to France, 36, 37; a Dane, in French service, 52; mentioned, 34, 36

Reconnaissances at battle of Arras, *T.*'s good judgment in, 73–75

Rethel, *T.* defeated at, 59; retaken by *T.*, 69

Retz, J. F. P. de Gondi, Cardinal de, quoted, 33, 34, 51, 52; on *T.*'s 'obscurity,' 150; quoted, 184, 235, 241

Rhine, crossing of the, 195; no Germans left on left bank of, 228

Richelieu, Armand Jean du Plessis, Cardinal de, his negotiations with the Duchesse de Bouillon which resulted in *T.*'s entering the

271

INDEX

French service, 3, 4; attempts to fulfil his promise to Louis XIII, 15, 16; as a result, had armies all over western Europe, 16; Bouillon's falling out with, over Soissons, 27, 28; his death, 30; result of his failure to select estates to be given the Bouillon family in exchange for Sedan, 30; *T.* refuses his niece's hand, 167; mentioned, 27, 29, 53, 124

Rochfort, M. de, 216

Rocroi, victory of, lost sight of, after Dutlingen, 37 and *n.*, 115

Rome, affair of Corsican Guard at, 129

Rosen, Lieutenant-General, heads mutiny among the Weimar troops, 47; how *T.* dealt with him, 47

Rospigliosi, Cardinal, 177, 185

Rouen, Monsieur de, his functions shorn after Mazarin's death, 104

Rousseau, Jean-J., 245

Royal Cavalry, quarrel in, 117–19

Roze, Comte de, 238

Ruvigny, M. de, 55, 144

Saint-Abre, M. de, criticizes *T.*'s military tactics, and *T.* advises him to carry his criticism to Court, 206, 207

Saint-Denis, *T.*'s body taken to, 241; monks of, celebrate a service for his friends, 242

Saint-Évremond, Seigneur de, quoted, 49, 50, 57, 117, 150, 189

Saint-Hilaire, M. de, père, 238, 239

Saint-Hilaire, M. de, jeune, quoted on *T.*'s death, 238, 239

Saint-Maurice, M. de, quoted on *T.*'s conversion, 178, 180

Saint-Simon, Duc de, *Memoirs*, quoted, 94, 99, 100, 134

Saint-Vénant, captured by *T.*, 80;

T. sacrifices his silver plate to pay arrears of the British troops, 80

Salis, Ferdinand de, at Arras, 76

Salzbach, *T.* forms his army and battle order near, 238

Sarpi, Fra Paolo, on the Council of Trent, *T.*'s reading of, 169

Saxe-Weimar, Bernard of, commands Army of Alsace, 22, 23; his decisive influence on *T.*'s character, 23, 24; *T.* quoted on, 23; favorite pupil of Gustavus Adolphus, 23; invited by Richelieu to enter French service, 24; *T.*'s indebtedness to, 26; mentioned, 39, 52

Schomberg, General Count von, 52, 103, 120, 124

Sedan, Principality of, one of the 'Sovereign States,' 4; turned over to France in return for the pardon of Bouillon for the Cinq-Mars affair, 29. *And see* 'Sovereign States'

Servien, M., letter of *T.* to, 37, 38

Sévigné, Mme. de, quoted, 147, 186, 187, 193, 235, 241, 242

Sinzheim, battle of, 230

Soissons, Bishop of, tries to convert *T.*, 168

Soissons, Comte de, harbored by Bouillon at Sedan on his falling-out with Richelieu, 27; killed at La Marfée, 28

Source, Count de, 103

'Sovereign States,' the, the Duchy of Bouillon and Principality of Sedan so-called, why the interest of France required them to be closely watched, 4; inherited by Charlotte de la Mark, 5; certain conditions, which were fulfilled by her marriage to La Tour d'Au-

272

INDEX

ice, 19; given command of a regiment and devoted himself to its organization, 19, 20; his first service in the Army of Italy, 20; until 1634, divided his time between France and Holland, 20; in 1634, definitively quitted the Dutch service, and served in the Army of Lorraine, 21; at the siege of La Motte, 21; made brigadier-general, 21; with the Army of the Rhine, his military talents first reveal themselves, in a hurried retreat, 21, 22; with the Army of Alsace, wounded at Saverne, 22; in the Army of Flanders (1637), siege of Landrecies, 22; again in the Army of Alsace under Bernard of Saxe-Weimar, 22; deeply influenced by him, 24; distinguishes himself at Ensisheim, 24; takes Brisach, 24; in Italy in 1639 and 1640, 24, 25; in command of the Army of Italy, 25; his progress in his profession, 25, 26; his anxiety about his brother's conduct, 26 ff.; obtains his brother's pardon for complicity in the Cinq-Mars conspiracy, 29; his confidence in Fabert, 29, 30

Did Mazarin try to convert him? 34; had he the far-reaching plans attributed to him by Mazarin? 34–36; his letters to his sister quoted, 34, 35; Mazarin first sent him to Italy, where he besieged and captured Trino, 36; made a marshal of France, 36; appointed to command the Army of Germany, 37; Mazarin's letter concerning him, 37, 38; his collaboration with Mazarin begins at this time, 38; d'Erlach offended by being placed under him, 39; tries to reconcile him, 39; his

great job of reorganization of the Army of Germany, 39, 40; reenforced by the Duc d'Enghien (Condé), 40; in 1645, recrosses the Rhine and goes into camp at Marienthal, where he was badly beaten by Mercy, 41; how he bore himself in adverse fortune, 41; offers to resign, 41; Mazarin's generous attitude, 41, 42; d'Enghien (Condé) takes over the command and beats Mercy at Nordlingen, 42; Condé's report on his conduct, and his on Condé's, 42; on Condé's retirement, brings the campaign to a close by taking Trèves, 43; rejoins troops at Mayence in 1646, 43; Mazarin orders him not to cross the Rhine to attack the Swedes, 43; later, on his own responsibility, crosses the river at Wesel, 43, 44; meets Mme. de Longueville at Wesel, 44; joining the Swedes, crosses the Main and marches to the Danube, 45; seizes Archduke Leopold's stores in Bavaria and drives him back to Austria, 46; forces Maximilian of Bavaria to accept the Peace of Ulm, 46; his campaign of 1646 praised more highly by Napoleon than any other, 46; ordered to send troops to Flanders against his judgment, 46; as he insisted, the German cavalry refused to follow him because their pay was overdue, 46; pursues mutineers under Rosen, 47; how he dealt with them, 47; ordered back into Germany because of defection of Duke of Bavaria, 47, 48; crosses the Rhine again and joins the Swedes, 48; drives Imperial army south of the Danube, 48; pursues in-

274

INDEX

joins those who sought to save him from the capital penalty, 111, 112; his activity found a fertile field in the reorganization of the army, 112; had been Colonel-General of Cavalry since 1657, 112; why it was a very important post, 112; the Secretaries of State for War were submissive to his military authority, 113; his relations with Le Tellier, 113; with Louvois, 113, 114; his task, to provide Louis XIV with the proper instrument to carry out his policy, 114; his work of reconstruction of the Cavalry, 114, 115; his disagreement with the King on the principle of selection of desirable recruits, 114, 115; sanctions the institution of brigadiers in the cavalry, 115; exerts himself most effectively in preparing troops for war, 116; believes in maintaining strict discipline, 116, 117; the incident of Montbas and Montpezat, 117–22; his name becomes prominent in connection with certain important military projects, 122; refuses to take part in any plan to dethrone the House of Nassau, 123; is frequently summoned by the King to meetings of his Council, 124; converses with him on foreign affairs, 124; his further part in the clandestine support given to Portugal, 124, 125; his friendship with Charles II of England, 126; Louis XIV forbids him to enter into personal correspondence with the King, 126; in the affair of the flag, 126; concerned in negotiations which lead to the reduction of the ransom for Dunkirk, 126; consulted by

Louis XIV concerning a treaty of commerce with England, 127, 128; tries to detach the Elector of Brandenburg from the Emperor, and to assure France of his friendship, 128, 129; his prevision of the future increase in power of Brandenburg, 129; at Rome, adjusts the affair of the Corsican Guard, 129; his opinion concerning the effect of Maria-Theresa's renunciation upon the sovereignty of the Low Countries, 130; strives to bring Sweden and Holland together, 130, 131; has friends or personal representatives everywhere, 131; continues to take part in important affairs of state despite the personal government of the King, 132; is subject, however, to unmistakable snubs, which prevent him from encroaching upon authority which nobody is allowed to share, 132; adapts himself readily to the new régime, 132

His life away from the army, 133 ff.; constant in his attendance on the King, 133, 134; firm in upholding his prerogatives, 133, 134; Saint-Simon's portrait, 134; lacked self-confidence, 134, 135; his houses in Paris, 135; not wealthy, 135, 136, 137; the King's gifts to him, 136; his simple mode of life in the army, 137; his generosity, 138; his kindness to his retainers, 139, 140; his manner toward his equals, 141; his relations with his wife, 142; his responsibility as head of the family, 142, 143; his friendships, Fabert, Condé, 143; his really intimate friends, amongst members of the Parliament and magistrates, 144,

277

INDEX